Higher education alternatives

Higher education alternatives

Edited by
Professor Michael D. Stephens and
Professor Gordon W. Roderick

Longman
London and New York

Longman Group Limited London

Associated companies, branches and representatives throughout the world

Published in the United States of America by Longman Inc., New York

First published 1978

Library of Congress Cataloging in Publication Data

Higher education alternatives.

   Includes index.
   1. Education, Higher — Addresses, essays, lectures.
2. Educational innovations — Addresses,
essays, lectures.   I. Stephens, Michael Dawson.
II. Roderick, Gordon Wayne.
LB2325.H482   378   77—21407
ISBN 0 582 48915 6

Set in IBM Journal 10 on 11pt
and printed in Great Britain by
Richard Clay (The Chaucer Press) Ltd,
Bungay, Suffolk

Contents

Part I   Some points for debate

Part II   Some responses

Acknowledgements

As with any collection of essays the number of people involved in the preparation of this book totalled far more than those listed as authors. Alas, space and editorial ignorance as to the names of all those who have in some way contributed means that we can only offer a very general 'thank you'. However, the one person we would wish to mention as having made a singular contribution in response to endless pleas for typing, re-typing, and collating is Miss Margaret Smith.

We are grateful to the following for permission to reproduce copyright material:

European Cultural Foundation for a table by Hequet, Verniers and Cerych in *Recent Student Flows in Higher Education*, 1976; Organization for Economic Cooperation and Development for Tables A, B and C from *Towards Mass Higher Education*, 1974; Routledge & Kegan Paul Ltd for an article entitled 'The Definition of Organizational Goals' by E. Gross from *The British Journal of Sociology*, September 1969; UNESCO for an extract from *Lifelong Education*, 1972, by the New Zealand National Commission.

Introduction

Professor Michael D. Stephens and Professor Gordon W. Roderick

'Universities cost money. They are being expanded to accommodate more students — without being required to show that they are places to which more and more students ought to go.'
(T. Burgess, *Education After School*, Penguin 1977, p. 115.)

In their discussion memorandum of 1975[1] the Dutch government summarized the feelings of a number of citizens in various countries with the statements 'The need for changes in the present system (of higher education) is acute' and 'Considerably more students have been flooding into the universities than will ever become scholars or research workers'. The report goes on to discuss two models of higher education, namely the British one where a non-university higher education sector exists alongside and separate from the university sector, and the American model of considerable diversity and no particular system. The document (p. 151) proposes that 'A way should be devised which will combine the British sense of reality . . . with American flexibility'. Whilst the Dutch report is an impressive exercise in trying to plan modern higher education it does tend to confirm Beloff's point in Chapter 7 of this book, 'how hard it is to think and act in defiance of the norms to which one is used'.

One major problem over modern higher education is a need to dismantle previous institutions and attitudes and create new ones in line with changed circumstances. Such is not to be other than under extreme revolutionary conditions and probably not then. Thus the higher education needs of the contemporary citizen have to be modified to fit traditional moulds or met by changing established institutions or bypassing them and creating parallel systems. The latter can be expected to appear in a variety of guises, and be both governmentally backed, such as the Open University in Britain, or without official patronage, such as the Free International University for Creativity and Interdisciplinary Research which appeared in a number of European countries in 1976–77.

Within higher education, universities in particular have a very powerful traditional role summarized by Levi[2] as 'to discover what we can of the nature of man and his universe'. This was put more specifically in London in 1975,[3] 'A commitment to higher standards suffuses all three basic aims which serve to define and distinguish the universities' role — teaching which inspires, research and its application which expands present boundaries of knowledge and understanding, and scholarship achieved by the work of men and women of considerable intellectual powers.' The same document (p. 4) makes the statement that 'university autonomy is vital'. This posture is challenged by our opening quotation and has both benefited and worked to the disadvantage of society. Universities have frequently been right in their conservatism, but have also been slow or unwilling to meet new needs within the community of which they are part. In the age of mass higher education their former exclusiveness has at times led them to ignore the full implications of serving the community's increasingly more numerous intellectual elite, let alone the full range of what Tress (Ch. 1) calls 'quaternary education'. The pace has been made by American education where the 'service' commitment of universities has been more highly developed than in almost all other countries. In contrast most European universities have been more interested in the issues of 'excellence' and the increasing of opportunities for young people to continue their education after school (end-on education). The responses of European universities and colleges to meeting community and economic needs have been much less than that of their American counterparts.

'Excellence', 'school-leaver access', and 'community and economic relevance' are often seen as being in conflict, although, as Burgess suggests (p. 113), 'There is no such thing as excellence, which is visible and attainable. It is just one way of saying which way we want to go. We want to improve, to excel; and it is not a quibble to recognize that excelling and excellence are comparative states.' Will the standard of 'academic excellence' suffer a decline in the face of increasing numbers of full-time undergraduates? Can higher education teaching staff escape from their narrow experience of the undergraduate schools to coping with, say, post-experience audiences and classes? Does the unleashing of a community's appetites for higher education mean the decline of research activities because of overstretched manpower resources? What of, as Perry points out (Ch. 8), academic credibility? The fears, both real and imagined, are endless and the dangers often significant. The proposed answers to the various higher education dilemmas are also legion and partly reflect the existing complexity of the field in many countries, and particularly those of Western Europe and North America. 'As universities in the twentieth century have grown countless new functions have been grafted on with little regard for how this growth of one function will affect the operation of others.'[4]

In the last 200 years the importance of education has increased beyond measure. As Vaizey[5] stated of British education, 'It is essential if we are to survive in a changing, technical and scientific age.' Such could not have been said of it in the eighteenth century. With the growth of its importance has gone an increasing commitment of resources with the inevitable greater governmental interest that follows. Since the Second World War in many of the developed countries investment in higher education has moved ahead at proportionately a greater pace than in other sectors of education. Higher education is always more expensive in per capita terms than the other areas of education. This has often meant that the search for educational alternatives has been more vigorous in higher education as the move from an exclusively elitist to a mass higher education service has taken place. Despite this search for alternatives higher education has remained slow to change. Where organizational innovation has taken place, as with the creation of polytechnics in Britain, the established models have imposed their image on the content of the new institutions' curriculum. 'By limiting universities or by universities limiting themselves to the scientific and the cultural, in the pattern of Humbolt's conventional disciplines, universities are in danger of becoming as sterile and as irrelevant as a parliament that limited its debates to constitutional matters, ignoring the economy, production and culture . . . we need more centres and devices of higher learning, other than the — at times — awful formality and laboriousness of universities and polytechnics.'[6]

In higher education terms since 1945 society has often seemed to be obsessed with quantity rather than with change. The great contribution has been that of 'more of the same'. The late Wayne Wilcox[7] took the United States model to explore the priorities in the light of the assumption that 'by 1985—90, the United States will probably have made the transition to almost universal higher education, including in its constituencies persons of rather indifferent intellectual ability and an increasing number of post-university adults, in new forms of higher re-education'. Wilcox listed four major functions for universities under such mass higher education pressure. Firstly, 'a growing population, increasingly concentrated in urban centres, with increasing leisure and less arduous physical work, will require the capacity for self-government and self-understanding to an ever greater degree. The intellect and the creative arts are likely to be much more important in the ordinary person's life, both as spectator and creator.' A second function would be in the area of the 'creation and protection of the independent intellect'. Thirdly, there would be the traditionally emphasized role of 'the generation of new knowledge'. The fourth function of universities is related to the previous one, namely 'the systematic diffusion of knowledge'. As Wilcox went on to stress 'in terms of historic university values, all four of these roles have ancient antecedents and there is a large measure of agreement, in academic circles at least, about their legitimacy'. However, what is missing is an educational framework which can serve them all with equal effectiveness. Perhaps the first function in particular has come off the worst in the listing of higher education priorities.

In meeting such roles institutions of higher education in all countries will face the already well-established problems such as growing demands versus limited resources, or the knowledge explosion overwhelming the possibilities for a very useful programme of study in the limited time available for all students. The ever more rapid increase in knowledge in all fields creates the full-time academic as a very real 'priest', whether reluctant or otherwise. Knowledge is power and only the professional academic has the time to fully acquire it. This has been emphasised because, as Crick[8] points out in the British model,

we appear to have chosen to lump an incredible amount of education, most of it compulsory, in the first two decades. And then it all comes to a stop. Well, not all, but expenditure on extra-mural, adult education and continuing education is very small indeed compared to that on Secondary

education. Indeed is very small, I am bound to add, compared to univer-
sity and polytechnic expenditure. If the budget is fixed, the resources
should be spread far more widely through different kinds of institutions
and throughout life.

In the light of an increasing realization that for many more people
education would have to take place throughout their lives, a number of
countries have become interested in 'Lifelong education' (called 'Permanent' education by Scheffknecht in Ch. 6 and 'Recurrent' education by
Fowler in Ch. 10). Much of the thinking behind this proposal was mulled
over by the New Zealand National Commission for the UNESCO
Committee on 'Lifelong education' which reported in 1972. They stated
(pp. 11–12):

'The Committee at various points in the report outlines some concepts
which it believes are essential for any system of lifelong education. We set
out these concepts at this point to emphasise the significant part they have
to play in lifelong education, both now and in the future.
'(a) Facilities for lifelong education should be available to all members of
*   our society as of right, and none should be excluded from them by*
*   economic hardship. Every effort should be made to ensure that*
*   everyone has ready access to a full range of educational opportunity in*
*   forms and at times which suit their needs.*
'(b) No form of education or training should be confined to those below a
*   specified or implied age limit. It should be possible for anyone at any*
*   age to re-enter any area of education, and to receive instruction*
*   adapted to his age and circumstances, even if this means providing*
*   "bridging courses" to enable adults to qualify for entry to more*
*   advanced courses. We consider that care should be taken to ensure*
*   that any formal qualifications required for entry are actually relevant*
*   and necessary to success in the course.*
'(c) In all fields of learning which are subject to change and development
*   (and it is now difficult to conceive of any which are not) continuing*
*   education must be made available to enable former students of the*
*   field to keep abreast of changes.*
'(d) Vocational and non-vocational education require equal emphasis
*   within the total pattern of lifelong education. The traditional distinc-*
*   tion between vocational and non-vocational education is becoming*
*   increasingly arbitrary and irrelevant and even where it can still be*
*   made, the areas of similarity are greater than the differences.*
'(e) In view of the rapidly increasing numbers of pupils who stay on
*   voluntarily in full-time education beyond the school leaving age, we*
*   feel that the notion of "compulsory education" is an outdated one.*
*   We look forward to the replacement of the idea of compulsion by one*
*   of the entitlement.*
'(f) Lifelong education, as a complex system serving individuals in a
*   complex society, requires the provision of integrated guidance and*
*   counselling services throughout life in personal, educational and*

vocational matters. These services, at their best, not only help individuals to get what they need from the education systems, but are also directly educational in themselves, being often a form of one to one teaching.

'(g) *In view of the importance of the quality of the early years of life to later development, and of the overwhelming importance of parental attitudes to the child's development during the early years, parent education must be given high priority.*

'(h) *From the secondary school onwards, learning and work should wherever possible be complementary rather than alternative and competing activities as they have generally been. This principle would involve part-time study and part-time work.*

'(i) *While continuing education will remain a part-time activity for most of its students and teachers, it should not on that account be seen as less important than other sectors. It should deploy a solid core of full-time staff no less professionally trained than staff in other areas of education. Training with suitable incentives to undertake it should also be available for part-time and voluntary staff.*

'(j) *The concept of university extension is now well established. It can be said, however, that all educational institutions have resources of staff, experience in certain special fields, or facilities, which could be used in the education of groups for which the institution does not primarily cater. In that sense all educational institutions have an actual or potential "extension" function. Examples would be the evening programmes of secondary schools (particularly the continuation classes), the use of primary-trained teachers for groups of slow learners in secondary schools, the education of mothers through the play centres, etc. One could go further and say that all institutions in society, of whatever kind, have a potential extension function, however limited and specialised. We feel that these kinds of extension should be explored and developed.'*

Many of the contributors to this volume start from an assumption that we must think of future education (in its formal sense of planned processes of learning undertaken by intent) as taking place throughout a citizen's whole life and not just during childhood and adolescence. The theme is also a central one in many of the most seminal national and international reports of the 'seventies such as Ontario's Report of the Commission on Post-Secondary Education *The Learning Society* (1972) or UNESCO's *Learning to Be* (1972). The Nineteenth UNESCO General Conference held in Nairobi in late 1976 in its Draft Medium-Term Plan reaffirmed the importance of Lifelong Higher Education, 'the higher education system can no longer restrict its function to catering for the needs of a specific age-group for a specific period; it must widen its scope to reach other people; it must extend its mission to the whole community'.

A wholehearted international acceptance of lifelong higher education is unlikely. In almost all countries with a well-established higher education system there is often disagreement on national objectives or priorities. Where governments do decide on some higher education objectives their priorities may seem related to a former age. The British politicians' demand for more applied scientists from its higher education system during the national debate of 1976–77 partly illustrates this. British universities needed such a priority in the nineteenth century, but the problem of the last quarter of the twentieth century may not be too small an output of, say, mechanical engineers from universities and polytechnics but a national inability to use the quite adequate numbers with greater effectiveness. Unlike many other developed countries the institutions of Britain, whether economic, social or political, are often at a loss as to how an applied scientist can be used to the most profit. Perhaps the dearth is in the production of social scientists to prepare Britain to change and match the so-called international rivals in the later twentieth century.

What society formally asks of its institutions of higher education is usually a need behind what it requires from them. As institutions of higher education, like all elitist organizations, are conservative, society can rarely look to them to rapidly change themselves. There is thus frequently a dysfunction between the existing roles of the institutions, the roles allocated to them by politicians, and the roles which society needs them to emphasize as a priority. This is as true of the higher education institutions of Europe or America as for the Third World of which Williams writes in Chapter 3.

When giving his inauguration address as founding president of the first of the modern American universities, Johns Hopkins, in 1876 Daniel Coit Gilman warned 'Universities easily fall into ruts. Almost every epoch requires a fresh start.' This danger is highlighted by Dominicé (Ch. 2) in his plea for more democratization of higher education; 'the opening of academic knowledge would become a valid alternative to the opening of the university's structure'.

The 'openness' of institutions of higher education relates to the complexity of goals found within them. Gross[9] has attempted a listing of possible goals within American universities. The first category Gross called 'Output Goals' which are expected to have some effect on the university and the society of which it is a part:

'1. Student-expressive: *Those goals which are reflected in the attempt to change the student's identity or character in some fundamental way.*

1.1 *Produce a student who, whatever else may be done to him, has had his intellect cultivated to the maximum.*

1.2 *Produce a well-rounded student, that is one whose physical, social, moral, intellectual and aesthetic potentialities have all been cultivated.*

1.3 *Make sure the student is permanently affected (in mind and spirit) by the great ideas of the great minds of history.*

1.4 *Assist students to develop objectivity about themselves and their beliefs and hence examine those beliefs critically.*

1.5 Develop the inner character of students so that they can make sound, correct moral choices.

'2. Student-instrumental: *Those goals which are reflected in the student's being equipped to do something specific for the society into which he will be entering, or to operate in a specific way in that society.*

2.1 Prepare students specifically for useful careers.

2.2 Provide the student with skills, attitudes, contacts, and experiences which maximize the likelihood of his occupying a high status in life and a position of leadership in society.

2.3 Train students in methods of scholarship and/or scientific research, and/or creative endeavour.

2.4 Make a good consumer of the student — a person who is elevated culturally, has good taste, and can make good consumption choices.

2.5 Produce a student who is able to perform his citizenship responsibilities effectively.

'3. Research: *Those goals which reflect the dedication to produce new knowledge or solve problems.*

3.1 Carry on pure research.

3.2 Carry on applied research

'4. Direct service: *Those goals which reflect the provision of services directly to the population outside of the university in any continuing sense (that is, not faculty, full-time students, or its own staffs). These services are provided because the university, as an organization, is better equipped than any other organization to provide these services.*

4.1 Provide special training for part-time adult students, through extension courses, special short courses, correspondence courses, etc.

4.2 Assist citizens directly through extension programmes, advice, consultation, and the provision of useful or needed facilities and services other than teaching.

4.3 Provide cultural leadership for the community through university-sponsored programmes in the arts, public lectures by distinguished persons, athletic events, and other performances, displays or celebrations which present the best of culture, popular or not.

4.4 Serve as a centre for the dissemination of new ideas that will change the society, whether those ideas are in science, literature, the arts, or politics.

4.5 Serve as a centre for the preservation of the cultural heritage.'

The second category is called 'Adaptation Goals' and demonstrates the need for the higher education institution concerned to come to terms with its milieu:

'1. *Ensure the continued confidence and hence support of those who contribute substantially (other than students and recipients of services) to the finances and other material resource needs of the university.*

'2. *Ensure the favourable appraisal of those who validate the quality of the programmes we offer (validating groups include accrediting bodies, professional societies, scholarly peers at other universities, and respected persons in intellectual or artistic circles).*

'3. *Educate to his utmost capacities every high school graduate who meets basic legal requirements for admission.*
'4. *Accommodate only students of high potential in terms of the specific strengths and emphases of this university.*
'5. *Orient ourselves to the satisfaction of the special needs and problems of the immediate geographical region.*
'6. *Keep costs down as low as possible through more efficient utilization of time, and space, reduction of course duplication, etc.*
'7. *Hold our staff in the face of inducements offered by other universities.'*

Thirdly, there are 'Management Goals' which relate to the leadership of the higher education institution:

' 1. *Make sure that salaries, teaching assignments, perquisites and privileges always reflect the contribution that the person involved is making to his own profession or discipline.*
' 2. *Involve faculty in the government of the university.*
' 3. *Involve students in the government of the university.*
' 4. *Make sure the university is run democratically insofar as that is feasible.*
' 5. *Keep harmony between departments or divisions of the university when such departments or divisions do not see eye to eye on important matters.*
' 6. *Make sure that salaries, teaching assignments, perquisites, and privileges always reflect the contribution that the person involved is making to the functioning of this university.*
' 7. *Emphasize undergraduate instruction even at the expense of the graduate programme.*
' 8. *Encourage students to go into graduate work.*
' 9. *To make sure the university is run by those selected according to their ability to attain the goals of the university in the most efficient manner possible.*
'10. *Make sure that on all important issues (not only curriculum), the will of the full-time faculty shall prevail.'*

There are also 'Motivation Goals' aimed at producing loyalty to the university on the part of its staff and students allied to a satisfactory level of morale:

'1. *Protect the faculty's right to academic freedom.*
'2. *Make this a place in which faculty have maximum opportunity to pursue their careers in a manner satisfactory to them by their own criteria.*
'3. *Provide a full round of student activities.*
'4. *Protect and facilitate the students' right to inquire into, investigate,*

and examine critically any idea or programme that they might get interested in.
'5. Protect and facilitate the students' right to advocate direct action of a political or social kind, and any attempts on their part to organize efforts to attain political or social goals.
'6. Develop loyalty on the part of the faculty and staff to the university, rather than only to their own jobs or professional concerns.
'7. Develop greater pride on the part of faculty, staff and students in their university and the things it stands for.'

Finally there are 'Positional Goals' aimed at maintaining an institution of higher education's prestige:

'1. Maintain top quality in all programmes we engage in.
'2. Maintain top quality in those programmes we feel to be especially important (other programmes being, of course, up to acceptable standards).
'3. Maintain a balanced level of quality across the whole range of programmes we engage in.
'4. Keep up to date and responsive.
'5. Increase the prestige of the university or, if you believe it is already extremely high, ensure maintenance of that prestige.
'6. Keep this place from becoming something different from what it is now; that is, preserve its peculiar emphases and point of view, its "character".'

It would seem inevitable that different institutions of higher education, and different people within a single institution, will give different emphasis to priorities within the above lists of goals. If we take the first category of Output Goals, it might be expected that the sub-divisions underlined by Holroyd and Loveridge (Ch. 4) would differ from those stressed by Kallen (Ch. 9). Similarly, someone who sees the study of, say, physics as a first commitment might well think differently about Adaptation Goals to those committed to the great use of the mass media in higher education (see Groombridge, Ch. 5).

Perhaps in the future what will dominate the selection of goals in higher education will be the increasing realization that it is one of the good things in life, despite the economic demands being more immediate, i.e. 'the time-scale for obsolescence in some important fields of knowledge developed in higher education had decreased from 100 years a century ago to 6 years by 1970'.[10] In Britain at present we have, for example, an extraordinary situation where the overwhelming bulk of the population still leaves education with no chance of ever sampling higher education. To take the more deprived half of our population, namely the female, a woman can expect to live to seventy-six years of age. She will be told to pay taxes towards a very expensive higher education provision for an elite of 18- to 21-year-olds. In all probability she herself will have left education at the minimum school-leaving age of sixteen years. Besides the stunning waste of human potential there seems a major injustice in asking that a citizen should only have eleven years of education and then sixty years without any more. Any volume on higher education alternatives must be obsessive over the key matter of how to make available the richness of higher education to the maximum number of citizens.

References

1. *Contours of a Future Education System in the Netherlands*, Ministry of Education and Science, The Hague, 1975, pp. 133 and 140.
2. E. H. Levi, *The University and the Modern Condition*, University of Chicago, 1968, p. 4.
3. Committee of Vice-Chancellors and Principals of the Universities of the United Kingdom, *Universities in a Period of Economic Crisis*, London, 1975, p. 1.
4. H. Livingstone, *The University: An Organisational Analysis*, Blackie, Glasgow, 1974, p. 26.
5. J. Vaizey, *Education for Tomorrow*, Pelican, Harmondsworth, 1970, p. 12.
6. B. Crick, 'Education and the Polity', Inaugural Lecture, Birkbeck College, 20 January 1977.
7. W. Wilcox, 'The University in the United States of America', in M. D. Stephens and G. W. Roderick (eds), *Universities for a Changing World*, David and Charles (Newton Abbot) and John Wiley (New York), 1975, pp. 34—50.
8. B. Crick, op. cit.
9. E. Gross, 'The definition of organizational goals', *British Journal of Sociology*, September 1969, pp. 277—94.
10. C. Ellwood, 'Adult learning today: A new role for the Universities?', *Sage Studies in Social & Educational Change* No. 4, London, 1976, pp. 12—13.

Part I

Some points for debate

Chapter 1

The universities' alternative in quaternary education *

Dr Ronald C. Tress

There is nothing static about university institutions, whether in the subjects which they teach, the research enquiries which they prosecute or the clientele which they serve. Slow moving they may be and certainly reluctant to contemplate as possible anything other than what they are doing at any one time. Yet they are capable of effecting remarkable changes in what they undertake whilst remaining true to their essential selves and there is no reason for assuming that a halt has been called to this evolutionary process. On the contrary, I believe that the outlines of a further stage are already visible.

The contention of this paper is that British universities — and they are not unique in the Western world in this regard — have become over-committed to 'tertiary education', the end-on education of those who have completed secondary education, the 18- to 25-year-olds; and that the time has come to shift their centre of gravity towards a greater participation in 'quaternary education', the stage which (in the phrase of the Russell report) is 'identifiably *adult*'.[1] I begin with questions about the purposes and habits of universities, to see how these have come to be set in and dominated by the interests of 'tertiary education'. From there I go on to consider the criticisms and dissatisfactions which are expressed with the universities' performance in this role. I then argue the claims of 'quaternary education', not only as a sensible resolution of some of the present difficulties but as the means of reasserting the primary function of universities in our society.

The purpose of universities

A university's primary and essential function is to acquire, to possess and to transmit scholarship. Lord Annan has written of two main functions: 'to promote through reflection and research the life of the mind' and 'to transmit high culture to each generation'.[2] I hesitate at the word, 'culture', but 'scholarship' I am sure about. A university is, first, a repository of scholarship. Secondly, it is a place where new acquisitions to scholarship are made and added to the corpus, partially and sometimes radically

---

* An earlier version of this paper constituted the Hartley Memorial Lecture, delivered in the University of Southampton on 15 October 1976.

reforming it. (The scholar's biggest obstacle to the grasping of new ideas is his difficulty in abandoning old ones.) Thirdly, it is a place where the tradition of scholarship is passed on from one generation of scholars to the next.

This is a blatantly elitist conception, both as regards what the members of a university staff should be doing and as regards why and whom they should teach. To speak of a repository of scholarship is to suggest something walled-up and safe, almost monastic, and this is deliberate. Professor Hugh Trevor-Roper has written,[3]

The early years of the eighth century, the years when the invasions of the Avars and the Lombards had been followed by the conquest of the Arabs, were indeed the darkest age of Europe. Outside the mutilated empire of Byzantium, European civilisation had by then shrunk to its smallest cell. It was the cell created by St Benedict in the days of Theodoric, the Gothic King of Italy: the monastic cell, with its self-contained economy, capable of survival in the oddest places and in the worst times, like a seed in the winter detritus of Nature. For this was the essential character of Benedictine monasticism. Every cell was independent. If one perished, others survived. If all but one perished, the system could yet be re-created from one survivor. And in fact, in those terrible years, all the most famous of the early monasteries would be destroyed, beginning with St Benedict's own monastery, Monte Cassino. It was in the monasteries of Ireland that fugitive scholars preserved a knowledge of the Latin and even of the Greek classics. It was in a monastery in Northumbria that the greatest scholar of his time, the greatest historian of the Middle Ages, the Venerable Bede, lived and wrote. And it was from the monasteries of Ireland and England, in the eighth and ninth centuries, that English and Irish fugitives would return to a devastated Europe. . . .

In the last quarter of the twentieth century when every subject has its own jet set and one may speak of 'invisible colleges' having global dimension, what bold academic would dare say that the Dark Ages might not recur, the books burned, the campuses occupied by troops?

'Scholarship' if it is less than 'culture' — the word of which I was earlier nervous — stands for more, I would point out, than research. And this is deliberate too. Scholarship, Sir Brian Flowers told the House of Commons Select Committee on Science and Technology, is 'the recognition of the place that new knowledge has in the general scheme of knowledge already acquired'.[4] And for that, as Dr Charles Carter had earlier observed, there must be scope for philosophical speculation and artistic creation as well as for discovering new knowledge, which is what is meant by engaging in research.[5]

But besides the acquisition and possession of scholarship, I have also spoken of its transmission, and here too, defining the university's *primary and essential function*, I have been elitist, restricting the essential requirement to transmission from scholars, renewing their own kind. In the first place, I believe this to be honest as a description, using as my criterion the views of my professional colleagues. Your academic enjoys three exquisite pleasures. One is to have brought to a successful conclusion some lengthy enquiry of his own. A second is to hear and be enthralled by some master expositor. The third is to discover some bright young pupil who — in contrast to the brilliant shadow boxer — has sought and wrestled with the material within his reach to produce what mentor recognizes as a new insight. This pleasure is the purest of the three, but it is undoubtedly elitist.

In the second place, however, I believe this elitist conception to be right. The repository must have its guardians and they must be sustained and renewed, in our twentieth-century technological society no less than in the Dark Ages — and no less, if we are to believe Dr Euan Mackie, than in the Bronze Age of 4,000 years ago when the peasant farmers in these islands 'were sufficiently well organized to support a small, elite group of intellectuals or "theocrats", astronomers and mathematicians who understood and seemed able to predict heavenly movements, and who were capable of fairly complicated arithmetic'.[6]

Having pinned down the *essential teaching function* of universities as being to reproduce their own kind, we must immediately go on to recognize a much *broader teaching habit* as their most common characteristic. It is this characteristic which has turned 'the groves of academe' into the Oxford and Cambridge Colleges, the redbrick and plate glass of our civic universities — and the extra-mural class. For it is a minority only of university teachers who are satisfied solely to teach just those who have the will to receive the transmissions of scholarship and the intellectual capacity to make it their own, becoming the heirs to the kingdom. The majority welcome a larger audience with whom they can share their enthusiasm for their subject, taking in the run-of-the-mill undergraduate tutorial as well as the stimulating postgraduate seminar and perhaps the extra-mural class in addition. Of course, there are those who want only to read and write, spending their time in their libraries or their research laboratories to which are admitted only their selected graduate students; those who accept other teaching only if they must, as a condition of their meal-ticket. But there are more who, while they gather research students around them and write articles which will be published only in their own learned journals and read only by their fellow scholars, at the same time welcome each new session of undergraduates.

We recognize, as an admired example of our own kind, the character portrayed in a recent *Times* obituary:[7]

His enthusiasm and devotion never faltered or flagged: each pupil felt himself the centre of his attention, all were swept away on the tidal wave of his ebullience, originality, and vinous hospitality. For him, each tutorial hour remained an adventure and a challenge: there were examiners (those natural enemies) to be outwitted and cut down in size, established theories to be toppled, whole sweeps of history to be rewritten for those who

*could stand the pace — and fill in the gaps — it was wonderfully exhilar-
ating.*

Courtenay Edward Stevens, to whom this obituary was a tribute, was an
Oxford don. He thus personified one brand of answer to the question to
which I now turn. If the broader teaching habit is a common characteristic
of universities but not an essential feature, there is an option about its
exercise. To whom shall the broader teaching be directed?

The Oxbridge answer is only one of a number of possible answers to this
question. It is not even the only English answer although such is the
historical dominance of Oxbridge to our ways of talking and thinking
about universities that people abroad are disposed to identify it as the
English answer and English university teachers at large are frequent contributors to the same belief. There is a proneness to talk of college staircases
and high tables as the apotheosis of university life and the personal tutorial
as the ideal teaching medium so that all other modes and practices are to
be counted as more or less inferior. In fact, we need to go no further than
north of the Scottish border for evidence to the contrary. The Oxbridge
system is a convenient marriage of two student elements which cannot
both be duplicated elsewhere: an intellectual elite — which I have deemed
essential — and a social elite, which is unique: a finishing school for the
sons of a governing class who also aim at reproducing themselves, to run
the government, the civil, diplomatic and colonial services, the judiciary
and clergy. Combine intellectual elite and social elite in a single system and
it is wise to emphasize a 'liberal education' as the hallmark of the curriculum. Furthermore, in that richly endowed context it is safe to say,
'teach the student and the subject will take care of itself'.

The English universities of today, however, are not typified by Oxford
and Cambridge even although their staffing may still be heavily and
influentially weighted from that source. The Scottish and, more powerfully
later, the Scottish and the German models not only provided an alternative
answer to that of Oxbridge to the question, to whom shall the broader
teaching be directed? It was their answer and not that of Oxbridge which
led to the nation-wide establishment of the civic universities whose
building up to predominance in the English system continues to this day.
England in the industrial revolution of the nineteenth century, as Professors Stephens and Roderick have reminded us,[8] was heavily reliant on
the products of the Scottish universities for the scientists, engineers and
medical men who were needed. The Scottish universities, though more
democratic, shared both the meritocratic outlook of the German and the
German's willingness to enter into the new sciences and technologies:
'That universities should be concerned with servicing the professional
needs of society was not a new idea and was indeed present during the
early days of the universities at Bologna and Padua, but the Germans
reaffirmed this function and extended the definition of 'professional'
needs to include the economic and industrial requirements of a techno-
logically based society.'

The pre-occupation with tertiary education

The reason that there are eighty-one university institutions in Great Britain today is not because it is reckoned that there is need for eighty-one separate repositories of scholarship to ensure the security of the tradition, or eighty-one separate groups for the efficient advancement of the corpus of scholarship, or eighty-one separate seminaries for the induction of the next generation of scholars. By these primary criteria the number is undoubtedly too great. It has resulted in too many libraries with too great a duplication of books and periodicals, too many research undertakings with inadequate support staff, and the number of postgraduate students too thinly dispersed for their own or their teachers' good. The reason for this number of institutions and their aggregate size — and the reason for the present-day criticisms of the structure to which I shall come in due course — is the near identification of what I have called the 'broader teaching habit' with tertiary education, the higher education of an 18- to 25-year-old age-group entering the universities directly following the primary and secondary education they have had in the schools.

The Robbins Report on Higher Education, in 1963, consolidated this near identification without ever seriously questioning either the historical motivations which had brought it about or its continuing appropriateness for the future. Thus, the Report's very brief summary of the growth in the university student population is a mere listing of Acts and statistical facts of the last 100 years with little reference to the sources of demand and none to the reasons which caused governments to meet it:[9]

First came the Forster Act of 1870 and the corresponding Scottish measure of 1872 which paved the way for free and universal elementary education. . . . There followed a great upsurge in the demand for secondary education. . . . As a result of [the Education Acts of 1944 and 1945] the school leaving age was raised to fifteen and free secondary education of all types was made available to all.

The improved opportunities for secondary education are largely responsible for the enormous growth in senior forms since the war. . . . These changes, reinforced by the steady rise in national prosperity, are now making their impact on the demand for higher education. . . .

Similarly, the Committee's tart dismissal of manpower forecasting takes for granted that the universities' concern is with the curricula of school-leavers and once-for-all. In such cases, consideration of manpower requirements must look ahead forty or more years and the Committee's conclusion for a technological society is then unchallengeable:[10] '. . . while it is possible, for a number of professions and over a short term, to calculate with a fair degree of precision what the national need for recruits will be, we have found no reliable basis for reckoning the totality of such needs over a long term.' The thought that greater versatility in adjusting to man power needs might be got if the timetable of the educational process were spread over the span of working life rather than concentrated at its threshold nowhere impinged upon the Committee's general argument.

'We have assumed as an axiom', declared the Robbins Report from the outset, 'that courses of higher education should be available for all those who are qualified by ability and attainment to pursue them and who wish to do so.'[11] After only a brief period of debate the universities of Great Britain have for the last decade been firmly committed to this axiom and to the Committee's own translation of it into statistical terms: that the undergraduate population should be determined by the number of school-leavers with a given A-level attainment and that the proportion of that number to be accepted should certainly not fall and, where possible, should rise.

Thus was the commitment to providing the bulk of tertiary higher education made total. Its consequence, besides the building of seven new universities (a decision taken by Government in 1958) and the translation into universities of nine colleges of advanced technology, has been a massive expansion for all existing institutions. There was, of course, a minority of resistant voices crying 'more means worse', that the quality of teaching would suffer. For the majority of university teachers, however, the commitment to large intakes had already been made.

While some diseconomies of scale were recognized — the loss of intimacy and easy intellectual exchange — the potential advantages of larger scale were more obvious and more telling. The exponential growth of knowledge called for greater specialization among teachers to keep abreast of their subjects and, in the laboratory subjects, larger units with more costly equipment for the prosecution of their research. Accepting more students would secure the finance to make these possible.

Measuring up to the growth in the scale of knowledge not only induced the academic staffs of universities to accept increasing numbers into tertiary education from the schools, however. It has had a further effect: a lengthening of the tertiary education curriculum. The notion has gone of students being brought to the frontier of most subjects by the time they have reached their third and final undergraduate year, able then to read and debate with their tutors the latest articles in their learned journals. The move to expand postgraduate teaching and to develop advanced courses as well as research programmes has followed. It marks the confluence of two streams of interest. First, there is the interest of the teachers. Attempts to extend first degree courses to a fourth year were quickly blocked by the refusal of Government to provide maintenance grants for students beyond the three-year period. The widening gap between undergraduate teaching and the subject-matter of the lecturer's own reading and research, therefore, meant that only by having post-graduate students could he 'teach his subject'. Secondly, there is the interest of the students, or at least — since the four-year undergraduate course for all was blocked — a proportion of them. As the Robbins Committee put it: 'the great extensions of knowledge in every field of study have made it impossible to provide adequate training for many careers within the limits of a three-year course.'[12]

So Governments have been willing, through the Research Councils and otherwise, to finance postgraduate 'research training'. And university departments have been eager, not only to absorb all the postgraduate research students on offer — for the laboratory subjects with their 'team' organization postgraduates are a cheap form of labour — but to invent 'taught Masters' courses of more or less relevance to the purposes which Robbins had in mind. The number of postgraduate students which any university department can muster has become a test of its intellectual standing among its peers.

The extent of this development in terms of student numbers can be readily set down. The Robbins Report recorded that, in 1961/62, there were 19,360 full-time postgraduate students in the universities of Great Britain; of these, 8,005 were following taught courses and 11,355 were occupied in research.[13] The corresponding total for 1974/75 was 47,870 (about 2½ times) with 23,767 on taught courses and 24,103 on research.[14] More significant even than these figures, however, is the doctrine which now surrounds them. I have earlier quoted the Robbins axiom that courses of higher education should be available for all those who are qualified by ability and attainment to pursue them and who wish to do so. But the reference then, in 1963, was to school-leavers and to first degrees. Now we have the words of eighteen of the most distinguished of our Vice-Chancellors and Principals reporting in July 1975 as a study group on postgraduate education:[15]

So far as undergraduate numbers are concerned the policy on which the universities plan and which is accepted by Government is clear. This policy requires that there should be a place in a first degree course for every student who is qualified for entry. . . . This principle is the expression at university level of a broader educational policy; that all young people should be enabled to develop their full potential, to go as far as their ability permits, and they themselves desire.

The ground on which universities take their stand must be that this principle applies as much at the postgraduate level as at any other. . . .

The commitment to tertiary education, continuous and end-on, from 18 to 25, from sixth form to Ph.D., is complete and entire.

Present discontents

At the beginning of this essay I distinguished between the essential teaching function of universities, the transmission of scholarship from one generation of scholars to the next, and what I called the broader teaching habit. The former was necessary to the continuance of universities in their primary role as the repositories of scholarship. The latter was an additional undertaking, readily accepted by universities but not of their essence and therefore optional· optional as to its undertaking at all in the first instance and certainly optional as to the form which the broader teaching habit might adopt. What has to be seen in the vast expansion of universities in number and size over the past 100 years and more is, first, a pre-emption of that option by the founders of new institutions. That pre-emption was never more than partial even by the founders, however, and the teachers appointed early asserted their academic rights. What has secondly to be seen, in the last quarter-century, is the surrender of the option by the teachers themselves.

The essential principle goes on being declaimed. Declared the Vice-Chancellors' Study Group to which I have earlier referred: 'The heart of the matter is the universities' responsibility for the maintenance and development of science and learning'.[16] Observed practice is very different. The whole of university policy is now dominated by the accepted form of the broader teaching habit, the universities' service to tertiary education, and this precisely measured by student numbers, full-time-equivalent numbers in neat packages of arts-based and science-based undergraduates and postgraduates. The Select Committee on Science and Technology reported in 1975,[17]

None of the evidence given to us by the UGC and the DES conflicts with the view that for all practical purposes student demand is the principal determinant both of the level of grants allocated by the DES to the UGC and of the allocation of funds to individual universities by the UGC, and that whatever the circumstances the universities are expected to give priority to their teaching activities at the expense, if necessary, of research.

Now comes the crunch, for the Select Committee continues: 'All the evidence suggests that this [the priority to teaching activities at the expense of research] is what is happening now, and this is what will continue to happen unless the rate of inflation is sharply reduced, or the funds available substantially increased'. That was in July 1975, since when the rate of inflation has not been sharply reduced but the funds available have diminished. University teachers having dutifully applied themselves to meeting the needs of society, and of a more equitable society as Robbins has presented it, now find themselves deprived of their just reward. The bargain has not been kept. Their primary function is threatened.

Nor is that all. The universities have become the object of public criticism for the teaching job that they have taken on, that they are too expensive and that their teaching lacks relevance: in short, as is said of other British enterprises, their prices are too high and their products are not what the customers want. In the case of British universities, however, the critical comparison is not with the work of foreign competitors. The flood of overseas students into Britain which has so alarmed the Government is a mark of the popularity of our scholastic wares and, in the terms of our balance of payments, add to the country's income from invisible exports and are not unprofitable according to Professor A. J. Brown.[18] The common comparison, however, is with alternative forms of higher education, in particular, the polytechnics.

The decision of the Labour Government in 1966 to establish 'the binary system' was compounded of a concern for costs and for control if all mass higher education was left to the universities, and to institutions which would acquire the status of universities, as Robbins has prescribed for the CATs.

Less is now heard of the comparative costs since studies have shown that, when like is compared with like, the polytechnics are not notably if at all cheaper to run, but the prior assumption dies hard in ministerial and official circles. The Select Committee on Science and Technology, for example, record a former Secretary of State for Education and Science opining 'that there has been for some years within the university system rather more scope for economies than in some other parts of the education system' referring to the staff–student ratio and his Deputy Secretary pursuing a similar line with respect to building programmes and to non-academic staffing.[19]

Criticism of the relevance of university teaching to the needs of our late twentieth-century society has a broader and more absolute base, less a matter of what the polytechnics may be doing better than of what the universities themselves, it is said, ought to be doing and are not. There is first, founded on dubious exercises in manpower planning,[20] the complaint that the universities are not turning out the requisite number of qse's (qualified scientists and engineers), a complaint now shifted to the schools which fail to provide the undergraduate intakes. There is, secondly, criticism of the postgraduate effort, well represented by the House of Commons Expenditure Committee reporting in 1973,[21] which excited the response of the Vice-Chancellors which I have earlier quoted:

At the heart of our proposals lies the conviction that too many talented young graduates find themselves slipping into postgraduate work for no clear reason (para. 103).

Of the 63,000 economically active people with postgraduate degrees in 1966, 20 per cent were university teachers, 20 per cent were teachers elsewhere in the educational system, 20 per cent were working as professional scientists and technologists and 13 per cent as doctors and dentists (para. 61).

We do not accept that postgraduate education should be mainly a means of training more teachers and more researchers. We do not accept that it should normally take place immediately after a first degree (para. 68).

So the universities of Great Britain, fourteen years after the Robbins Report and after an unprecedented expansion in size and number, find themselves unloved and ill-served. Where should they go from here? I suggest a return to first principles.

First principles and tertiary education

I began this paper with the statement that a university's primary and essential function was first to be a repository of scholarship, secondly to be a place where new acquisitions to scholarship are made and added to the corpus, and thirdly a place where the tradition of scholarship is passed on from one generation of scholars to the next. The transmission of scholarship as an *obligation* on universities I thus limited to the renewal by scholars of their own kind. Transmission beyond those select ranks was, in principle, a matter of choice. The 'broader teaching habit', the other phrase I used, might be of the *bene esse* of universities, but it was not of the *esse*; it was of their well-being, not their being.

If nothing else has come out of my survey so far, however, one thing is certain. For the future well-being of the universities a major commitment to broader teaching has become inescapable. First, as I have indicated, the financing of university activity on anything like its present scale depends upon it. Britain's eighty-one university institutions are paid to teach and the majority of them would not exist but for that purpose. Secondly, however, and this is also a point I made earlier, the majority of university teachers want to teach and want to teach to a wider circle than just potential professors or fellows of All Souls'. It may have been the experience of Cardinal Newman that 'to discover and to teach are distinct functions: they are also distinct gifts, and not commonly found united in the same person'.[22] I am not unaware of examples which would support his final phrase. Nevertheless, I do not believe it of the majority of academic staffs. The Association of University Teachers is the profession's own choice of identification, coined long before university teaching became the mass teaching that it is today and long before the Association itself became a trade union.

But there is a third reason for the broader teaching undertaking and that vital to the universities' well-being. There is an intellectual inheritance to be acquired, conserved, added to and passed on and these are the universities' first duties. The ease of their performance, however, depends a good deal upon the environment in which they operate. My introduction of the eighth-century Benedictines was not just a glint of colour in an otherwise grey landscape. They are relevant here. They had no choice but to retreat from what were hostile, destructive surroundings. The present-day environment of our universities is only mildly hostile, and there are opportunities, if we will seize them, for bringing about favourable change.

The pursuit of scholarship requires a freedom to enquire and to question. The exercise of that freedom is, unfortunately, not all accomplishable by armchair speculation. It is costly in books, in apparatus, in personal travel and interchange as well as in the time of its practitioners. So it needs the support of society for its resources. At the same time, it is of its nature dangerous to that society because it is disturbing: it challenges conventional wisdom and disrupts established practices. As Dr Wayne Wilcox, contemplating the future of universities in the United States, has put it:[23]

Universities, whether elite, practical or socially responsive, have a common interest in sustaining the kind of society in which inquiry and intellectual/ artistic independence is protected. No other major social institution has such an interest. The suborning of truth is a historical tendency to all self-interested institutions, whether clerical, political or commercial. In each case, the influential of any organisation are pursuing normative values — the true faith, national interest, profit — but they are calculating in the short term as well as the narrow field. Artists and intellectuals also have a narrow interest around a prime value — truth and its expression, as best as they can see it — and in an organised and collectivist world, the only secure major forum for the expression of such a value is the free university.

So universities must themselves *promote* the kind of society which is favourable to their objectives and practices and *court* those in the existing society who are, or might be, their friends. There are numerous ways in which this promotion can be done: the participation by their members in the everyday affairs of society and particularly where they can offer recognized expert help; the undertaking of research enquiries of immediate benefit if these are voluntarily entered into without sacrifice of the performers' autonomy and commitment; above all — and here I return to the mainstream of my argument — through the universities' broad teaching undertaking, but *designed to a common end*.

The universities should not seek a priority hold on, still less a monopoly of, the 'higher education' component of tertiary education. It is, of course, their task to choose and sustain the succession of scholars. There is much else in the general undergraduate field which they must continue to provide. There is more in the immediate postgraduate field. But the frontier of knowledge has moved forward and it is both society's interest and the universities' interest that the frontier of teaching should move with it. The new territory to be occupied lies in post-experience education, adult education, what I have called in my title, quaternary education. Such will be my argument.

Only in the case of the medical professions is there complete dependence upon the universities for the generality of school-leavers' higher education. Solicitors and accountants train under articles with practising principals; so do surveyors. Would-be barristers read for the bar in chambers. Engineers may or may not have embarked on their careers with a university degree. Universities may teach art history, musicology and the study of drama; school-leavers go to art schools to learn painting and sculpture, to colleges of music to become composers or performers, to theatre schools to learn acting and stage production. The universities really come into their own in providing the less specific courses of tertiary study, in the arts, sciences and social sciences.

The school-leaver has a choice of institutions. At the time of the Robbins Report in 1963 it was between the universities, colleges of advanced technology, technical colleges and colleges of education. Now, a new structure is being built up. At the latest count (1976), besides the 81 university institutions (44 universities) already referred to, there are 30 polytechnics, 27 colleges of education, 44 colleges of higher education and an almost unknown number of colleges of further education which may or may not include some degree teaching in their offers.

Now, I hope that no one will accuse me, as a member of the Houghton Committee of Inquiry into Teachers' Pay of being ungenerous towards the polytechnics. I have nevertheless to confess difficulty in either understanding or, if I understand, appreciating the role ascribed to them by their own Committee of Directors. Their policy statement of 1974 has as its title *Many Arts, Many Skills*, and emphasizes the wide span of educational provision which the polytechnics undertake, the wide range of entry qualifications which admit their students and the wide range, from higher technician level to higher degree to which their qualifications lead. This part of their statement I recognize and — saving some comments on the way in which the term 'level of work' is used, about which I have written elsewhere[24] — I applaud the undertaking. My puzzlement comes later, in the invocation of the word 'professionalism' as characterizing their purpose and their mode of teaching:[25] 'The role of the polytechnics is the professional teaching of the practical arts, the many arts and many skills, at all levels of scholarship which constitute higher education and are required by modern professionalism'.

I have already pointed out by implication that the polytechnics have no place in one major field of professional training, that of medicine. Their involvement in the training of school-teachers is only just beginning, as a result of take-overs of colleges of education. They certainly do not have exclusive commitments to engineering, law or theology, to quote ready instances where professional practice certificates are required. Nor can I accept the Directors' statement about professionalism in their teaching, as constituting any distinguishing mark. Every good teacher at every level, from kindergarten upwards and outwards, knows that to teach he must take that which in broad terms he knows he has to impart, first make his material his own possession and then assist his pupil to possess it in turn and in the pupil's, not the teacher's, own way. Professionalism of that sort is required at all ages and at all levels. What differs is the depth of scholarship at which the activity takes place: how much material there is to be possessed.

Here I can re-unite with the Polytechnic Directors:[26]

... students do not readily classify themselves into university and polytechnic types. There may be a small number clearly committed to a future in scholarship for whom a university is very much the right choice; there may be some with a clear commitment to a particular vocation best served by attendance at a polytechnic or at a college; but the majority are young people in search of a broad educational experience to enable them to develop personally and culturally as well as vocationally, and who could well attend either type of institution.

I agree, and my conclusion follows. The polytechnics and the colleges of higher education are bidding for more school-leavers. The universities should let them go. It does not make either economic or educational sense for the institutions on the public side of the binary line to have unfilled undergraduate places. The first and hardest lesson which universities have to learn about zero-growth is that development has to proceed by substitution, not by addition. University teachers can no longer afford to say, we will do these new things if we are given more resources; they must learn to say, we will do these new things instead of these old things. The universities should welcome a switch of school-leaver numbers to the polytechnics and colleges, because they have other, and more adventurous things to do.

The special character of the universities to be exploited is that they are repositories of scholarship and places especially where scholarship is advanced. In speaking of 'more adventurous things to do', however, I do not mean a shift to more postgraduate education if that is simply end-on to the undergraduate curriculum, what I have described as extended tertiary education. Here, as with first degree study, we seek an optimal use of resources. We should accept, therefore, neither the exaggeration of the House of Commons Expenditure Committee that 'postgraduate education should normally be taken after a period of employment'[27] nor the myopia of the Vice-Chancellors' Study Group who see part-time postgraduate students as unfortunates 'whose family commitments, or other circumstances, make full-time study impossible'.[28]

If, as Government and Expenditure Committee (if not the Vice-Chancellors) are broadly agreed, 'postgraduate education should be shaped, not by student demand alone, but principally by the needs of the economy and of society as a whole',[29] then there is certainly scope and necessity for both end-on postgraduate research and end-on 'taught-Masters' courses, whatever the MPs may go on to say. As the Government's reply to the Expenditure Committee has it: 'In some areas of study such as mathematics or non-clinical medical research, there may be positive disadvantage in a break after the first degree'.[30]

Furthermore, there *are* careers calling for young postgraduates, and, in the Government's words:[31]

A certain looseness of fit is necessary not only because the knowledge and techniques for bringing about a close match are lacking, but also to allow for the fact that some of the best postgraduates put their education and training to good use in ways which it is impossible to predict or relate to any mere extrapolation of the existing job market.

All that admitted, however, I believe that the central *positive* argument of the Expenditure Committee remains:[32] 'Every encouragement should be offered . . . to post-experience students who wish to take vocational courses, either full-time or part-time. . . . Nor would we want to discourage the provision of non-vocational taught courses for post-experience students, particularly part-time courses.'

Quaternary education

If knowledge is expanding explosively, making old knowledge obsolete, the effect upon the pattern of employment is too drastic to leave the adaptation of the nation's manpower simply to the rate at which new entrants to the workforce replace those going into retirement. What is the half-life of contemporary knowledge? In many fields at the present day it is well short of a man's working years. If we are not to have out-of-date people as well as out-of-date machines, there must be re-training as well as training; there must be continuing education. Furthermore, there are some technological developments which are best left to the coming generation because their seniors are too old to learn new tricks. But there are other developments which are best put into the hands of persons with experience behind them: in areas of management, for example, experience of people can be as important to successful innovation as is knowledge of things.

The most radical thoughts arising from these observations would start with reform of the schools. The practical formulations of *education permanente* in Continental Europe most often have a plain vocational purpose, but the philosophy goes deeper. It is that a national educational system should have as its field the *lifelong learning needs* of its citizens. And once it is accepted that there is no school-leaving age, except as the conclusion to the first full-time phase, then the curriculum does not have to be crammed in at a rate aiming at completion somewhere between the ages of 16 and 25. It can be revised to take account of a lifetime spread, the initial full-time phase to be followed by a succession of shorter periods of full-time and part-time study sandwiched between, or accompanying, periods of gainful occupation. These periods would be optional, and designed to meet people's own recognition of their discontinuous needs as they arise, but not just from their vocational life; from their personal or social life as well.

Like the Open University's committee which has lately reviewed what it calls 'continuing education', however, I shall not adopt 'the view that the only valid schemes of continuing education are those which require the prior radical revision or transformation of the educational system or of society as a whole before they can be achieved'.[33] My concern in any case is with the farther end of the spectrum, the frontier where the universities may operate. I shall rely upon present-day examples.

First, two substantial reports on higher education since that of the Robbins Committee have given primary attention to continuing professional education and training. In the report of the Royal Commission on Medical Education, in 1968, the chapter on postgraduate education and training preceded that on the undergraduate medical course. Lord Todd and his colleagues wrote:[34]

We think that doctors in every branch of medicine now need several years' postgraduate training, and in view of the speed at which medicine and medical care are advancing no doctor should lack the opportunity at any time in his career. Postgraduate medical education should therefore be extended and reorganised so as to provide a systematic and rational progress from basic qualification to the appropriate level of career competence, and to maintain that competence thereafter.

This statement is the more impressive in that, at the time, medical education and training did not go beyond the intern year. The retraining of school-teachers was better provided for. Nevertheless, it is notable that the James Committee enquiring into teacher education and training in 1972 put its chapter on the 'third cycle' before those on the 'second cycle' (pre-service training and education) and the 'first cycle' (the DipHE):[35] 'The third cycle comprehends the whole range of activities by which teachers can extend their personal education, develop their professional competence and improve their understanding of educational principles and techniques. . . . For this large and complex field, it is clear that "inservice training", however convenient as shorthand, is a very misleading term'. The medical undertaking represented by the Todd Commission's programme falls wholly upon the universities' postgraduate medical schools. Lord James's third cycle waits upon the settlement of the Area Training Organization (ATO) reforms.

These two are both vocational sources of demands where the participants will be sponsored by their employers. As a third such instance one might look to business and public administration. The civil service, besides developing its own staff college, makes fair use of university postgraduate courses for its training programmes. In the case of 'management education', however, despite the advent of the London and Manchester Business Schools, the university contribution has been mostly in MA/MSc courses, the bulk of the entrants to which have gone straight from their first degrees, their studies financed by Research Council postgraduate awards rather than by sponsoring employers. Many of the larger undertakings have their own permanent training establishments and their external placements are generally for specialized courses of short duration aimed at serving some immediate establishment need of a more or less technical character. There seems no reason to amend the conclusion of a government-sponsored survey in 1968 that the call on the university sector would continue to be small.[36]

But the reference is to students sponsored by employers. Let me, from the immediate experience of Birkbeck College, give two illustrations of vocational, but student-generated demand. Seven or eight years ago, it was practicable for the College's computer science department to have students from several academic levels — service teaching, first degrees, taught Master's courses — all covering much the same ground. The principal distinction between Bachelor's degree students and Master's degree students wasn't whether they had studied computer science previously; both groups were new to the discipline. The distinction was whether or not they had a degree in another subject. Not so today. The majority now hold degrees in computer science; but, with theories and techniques developing, they need to go on studying to keep up to date, not only with the capabilities of the newest machines but with the capabilities of the new recruits to their profession who are coming up behind them. The College's undertaking is now not only wholly post-graduate but specializing in a particular area of the subject, deriving from the department's own researches on data processing and information systems. It is frontier teaching.

Secondly, Birkbeck College's psychology department has a high demand for its first degrees. The bulk of the entry consists of professionally quali-fied teachers and social workers who did some psychology in their early training. Now, as the result of developments in national policy, new educa-tional and social service professions are being established. These people have the background and personal experiences fitting them for these posts but they lack mastery of the subject. The College is currently meeting that need at the first degree level, but very shortly the demand will move to being postgraduate as the new professions fill up and careers are under way. It will become frontier teaching.

The motives which drive mature men and women to embark upon inten-sive study of their own volition — which will generally mean in their spare time — are various. For the kind of course I have spoken of so far, how-ever, I suspect a fairly high correlation between their chosen subjects of advanced study and what they envisage as their employment prospects. Either they aim to *improve* their position within their current occupation or in one closely allied to it. Or else they foresee declining opportunities in their present line — at best, a low-earnings profile, at worst redundancy — and seek to *adapt* their innate capabilities to a new and more promising line of work. In the first case, the fact that they have the energy for study, on top of a day's work, is itself demonstrative that their abilities are at present under-utilized. In the second case, an element of desperation may add to their drive.

But what is the relationship between intellectual attainment and employment prospects? It is certainly not a one-for-one correspondence. The successful industrial manager must have a way with men as well as with money. The school-teacher must know his pupils as well as his subject. A more substantial move of universities into the quaternary educa-tion of the mature student will require an increased concern for human development besides serving the calls of career development. It is a criticism of the British business schools which have grown up within the shadow of the universities that they have concentrated upon adding to their students' knowledge and command of techniques and, less justifiably than the universities, are disposed to neglect the part played in a large number of life situations by individual behaviour and human relations as such. Yet these are matters which, as often as intellectual obsolescence, can mar a man's career. If universities will properly apply themselves to the frontier areas of quaternary education there will be plenty of oppor-tunities, indeed a need, for an accompanying counselling service: the

'English' university model should be united with the 'German' or the 'Scottish'.

But we should not see the total quaternary undertaking solely in vocational terms, any more, one is happy to note, than did the Expenditure Committee. Reference to personal counselling reminds us that we are dealing with whole persons, nor mere units of economic manpower. The point has two kinds of significance. First, as the Russell Committee pointed out, while the rate of accretion of new knowledge as it bears upon those already highly educated is frequently commented upon, the extent to which new knowledge has to be absorbed by the common man in his daily life goes unremarked:[37] 'The changing rights and duties . . . of the citizen, the consumer, the road user, the trade unionist, the recipient of welfare benefit, the householder, or the parent, are examples where adult education has barely begun. . . .' Secondly, man cannot live by bread alone. The Russell Report is right to point out that: 'leisure frequently presents itself in unwelcome forms — short time, redundancy, retirement, long-term incapacity or unemployment — which in a work-oriented society can be deeply destructive of the personality and self-respect'. There is still, more now than ever for the mass of population, 'the leisure, properly so-called, of individual choice and personal cultivation'.[38]

Subjects like history, politics, philosophy and English literature are the traditional core of English adult education and of the universities' contribution thereto. Nor did the scholars of yesteryear deem it too demanding of their time, still less beneath their dignity, to engage in such activity. Under the pressures of meeting the demands of tertiary education, the habit among university teachers at large has declined and the task has been left increasingly to resident extra-mural specialists and their associates. A shift in the balance of the universities towards quaternary education should include a revival of the extra-mural tradition and its extension to all the arts and sciences. To become thus more deeply involved in adult education within their communities, the universities do not need to compete with the offerings of the further education colleges, but to complement them, and at the universities' own special standard. A joint working party of the Vice-Chancellors' Committee and the Universities Council for Adult Education has summed up that standard:[39] 'work which demands a level of teaching and learning characteristic of universities, which fully engages the minds of their teaching staff and which gives opportunities for study of a quality (if not necessarily the same total subject matter) associated with degree awards'. There are extra-mural constituents among the quaternary audience, as well as post-experience graduates, alive to news of happenings at the scholarly frontiers.

In quaternary education there are matters in plenty to exercise the knowledge, philosophical speculation and artistic creation which — returning to the words of Dr Carter quoted earlier — are the constituents of true scholarship, for the sake of which universities exist. In undertaking them the broad teaching habit of the universities will be more assuredly related to their primary, essential purpose.

References

1. *Adult Education: A Plan for Development* (the Russell Report), Report by a Committee of Enquiry appointed by the Secretary of State for Education and Science under the Chairmanship of Sir Lionel Russell CBE, HMSO, 1973, para. 47.
2. In M. D. Stephens and G. W. Roderick (eds), *Universities for a Changing World*, David and Charles, 1975, p. 19.
3. H. Trevor-Roper, *The Rise of Christian Europe*, Thames and Hudson, 1966, pp. 85—9.
4. Quoted in *Scientific Research in British Universities* (Second Report of the Select Committee on Science and Technology, Session 1974—75), para. 41.
5. In G. Brosan, C. Carter, R. Layard, P. Venables and G. Williams, *Patterns and Policies in Higher Education*, Penguin, 1971, p. 78.
6. Address by Dr Euan Mackie, assistant keeper at the Hunterian Museum, Glasgow, to the International Union of Prehistoric and Protohistoric Scientists, Nice, 1976 as reported in *The Sunday Times*, 19 September 1976.
7. Obituary of Mr C. E. Stevens, *The Times*.
8. M. D. Stephens and G. W. Roderick, op. cit., pp. 8—9.
9. *Higher Education* (the Robbins Report), Report of the Committee appointed by the Prime Minister under the Chairmanship of Lord Robbins, 1961—63 (Cmnd 2154, 1963) paras 41—2.
10. Ibid., para. 13.4.
11. Ibid., para. 31.
12. Ibid., para. 293
13. Ibid., Appendix Two(A), Table 43.
14. Expenditure Committee, Government Observations on Third Report, Session 1973—74, *Postgraduate Education* (Cmnd 6611, 1976), para. 9.
15. Committee of Vice-Chancellors and Principals, *Postgraduate Education, Report of a Study Group* (1975), paras 69—70.
16. Ibid., para. 7.
17. *Scientific Research in British Universities*, para. 67.
18. Committee of Vice-Chancellors and Principals and University Grants Committee, *Tuition Fees*, Interim Report of a Joint Working Party (1975), paras 26—32.
19. *Scientific Research in British Universities*, para. 26.
20. K. G. Gannicott and M. Blaug, 'Manpower Forecasting since Robbins: a Science Lobby in Action', *Higher Education Review*, Vol. 2, No. 1 (Sept. 1969).
21. *Postgraduate Education* (Cmnd 6611), paras 103, 61 and 68 as indicated.
22. J. H. Newman, *On the Scope and Nature of University Education* (1859), Preface.
24. R. Tress, 'Levels of Work', *The Times Higher Education Supplement*, April 1975.
25. Committee of Directors of Polytechnics, *Many Arts, Many Skills*, The Polytechnic Policy, and requirements for its fulfilment (1974), para. 27.
26. Ibid., para. 36.
27. *Postgraduate Education* (Cmnd 6611), para. 93.
28. *Postgraduate Education, Report of a Study Group*, para. 60.
29. *Postgraduate Education* (Cmnd 6611), para. 6.
30. Ibid., para. 11.
31. Ibid., para. 7.
32. Ibid., para. 98.
33. The Open University, Committee on Continuing Education, *Interim Report* (1976), para. 23.
34. Royal Commission on Medical Education 1965—68, *Report* (Cmnd 3569 1968), para. 59.
35. Department of Education and Science, *Teacher Education and Training* (1972), para. 2.2.
36. National Economic Development Office, *Management Education in the*

1970s: Growth and Issues, A report by Professor Harold Rose, HMSO, 1970.
37. Russell Report, para. 43.
38. Ibid., para. 36.
39. Joint Working Party of the Vice-Chancellors' Committee and the Universities Council for Adult Education, *Report on the Future Scope and Organisation of Adult and Continuing Education in Universities* (1974), para. 2.

Chapter 2

How open should the university be?

Dr P. Dominicé

Access to the university

Like schools and most other educational institutions, the university in Europe is both the symbol of the traditional culture which has dominated Western civilization and the scene of many transformations, some of which have led to the emergence of innovations.

A number of authors have stressed the class privileges which the university reflects. They have demonstrated that the nature of its population confirms the inequality of chances for access to higher education. Certain writers have criticized the lack of interaction between university research or teaching and social needs or daily problems with which our society is confronted. With regard to these problems, the university does not need to be brought to trial once again.

But the question that remains unresolved is that of knowing whether in the future it would be advisable to open the university to new publics by creating more flexible admissions procedures and reorganizing its programmes: or whether, on the contrary, it is preferable to give priority to the development of other institutions of higher education and, above all, to a more systematic extension of adult education in all areas possible.

Reforms and their limits

If and when it is to recognize its responsibility to contribute more directly to adult education, the university will have to redefine its structures.

In many universities, notably in Switzerland, the reforms that were introduced in the wake of the student protest movements of the 'sixties may now be understood to be the result of a series of social regulatory mechanisms that had become necessary, given the changes the society had undergone during the last years. Despite the conflicting pressures brought to bear on the university by its critics, it has in general manoeuvred in a protectionist manner, preserving its structures intact.

Efforts to open the university to adults remain blocked because the promoters of these new programmes do not know clearly whether they hope simply to diversify the university's publics, or, more ambitiously, to tackle the whole structure. At the moment, while the university has learned to tolerate these new educational activities, it has also managed to keep them marginal to its more traditional interests.

In the case of new experiments carried out in Western Europe recently, such as those at Roskilde in Denmark[1] or at Vincennes in France, no broader fundamental changes were brought about.[2] As interesting as these innovations are educationally or with respect to theoretical products, they have had no effect on the more global organization of university teaching and research in the countries where they appeared.

What is at stake in university research and teaching

In order better to grasp the tension existing between tradition and innovation within the university, it would normally be necessary to enter into a discussion of the social and political conditions influencing the university structure within its particular context. However, I wish to address myself here to *the problem of knowledge* which, upon examination, may be found to provide one of the keys to considering the very problem of access to the university or other institutions of higher education.

In this perspective, the basic questions seem to be the following: Does the university have a special responsibility in the production of theoretical models and scientific knowledge? Should research be emphasized, and should researchers be given sole responsibility for defining the fields of investigation? Is it, to the contrary, preferable to orient university research and teaching according to questions emerging more or less explicitly from different social groups or according to the demands of the State? In the latter case, should access to the knowledge normally diffused at the university be facilitated, and should the university's public service role be considered more seriously? Is it possible for the university's students or its diverse adult populations to collaborate in an original way in real intellectual creation? These are complex questions. I make no pretence of providing definitive answers in this text, but wish, rather, to frame the problem in such a way that these questions may be seen in proper perspective. *To open the university is also, and perhaps principally, to ask about the nature and the end of the knowledge by which the university can and must define itself.*

Conscious of the fact that no university reform can be conceived independently of the economic, political and ideological factors weighing on it, I have no intention of redefining the place and function of the university. Instead, my aim is to suggest both strategical orientation and experimentation possibilities which, serving here as illustration, might — in the case of real political change — designate the direction in which deeper transformations might proceed. It is very clear that due to present institutional difficulties, these fields of experimentation are not generalizable. They do not constitute alternatives to the present structure of the university, but indicate an educational perspective founded on a new concept of knowledge and consequently, on a new definition of education.

Institutional resistance to change

The liberties that university instructors take in a few particular sectors are only possible in so far as the university fully satisfies the requirements which more and more justify its function in society: ideological training of future executives, diffusion of the scientific skills required for professional qualification, research in scientific fields requiring new applications. Several modifications have, of course, been introduced in the last few years: new courses or diplomas, interdisciplinary programmes, wider access to certain programmes, more rationalized curricula, new efforts at evaluation.

But as soon as these changes go beyond the limits prescribed by institutional statutes and mental attitudes, they are tolerated only on account of their partial and frequently temporary character. The opening of the university to the city, which in Geneva took place through the creation of a Senior Citizens' University, and of degrees in social policy or human ecology, is only accepted in so far as these activities are juxtaposed to the general programme and do not modify it. In other words, the model can take a few innovations as long as its working equilibrium is not perturbed.

Because of budgetary restrictions imposed upon it, the university must now defend itself to survive. Basic research, when its utility is not immediately evident, is not always accepted. Critical analysis of the social system is scarcely tolerated. For example, departments of colleges, such as education or architecture, may be considered subversive, especially if they venture to propose alternatives to current practice in the schools or to on-going urban development.

The absence of real reforms in secondary schools encourages the university to prolong scholastic methods of learning.[3] With the exception of certain scientific and medical sectors, there is scarcely any interaction between the knowledge diffused at the university and its practical application. In most cases, teachers are not addressing interlocutors who confront them with concrete knowledge of a particular social reality or professional field. When instructors do take a role outside the university context, they most often do so as experts. How then could they be sensitive to other needs than those they have deemed worthy of priority from the sanctity of their offices or laboratories?

Intellectual production and university constraints

As it is obvious that pressures moulding the university actually do end in establishing course contents and justifying pedagogical approaches, it would be illusory to deal with the question of learning and to envisage another strategical orientation without briefly evoking the constraints placed on intellectual production at the university.

1. University scholarship is abusively confined to *scientific knowledge*, to the detriment of a broader view of culture and a valorization of ethical reflection and artistic creation. Moreover, scientific production, as it

exists in the exact sciences, tends to become the model to which social research is expected to conform today. Unless it can guarantee objectivity, proper variable control and statistical validity, social research is said to be speculative, and its assembled data to lack sufficient reliability. This normative pressure particularly affects research in education, which never quite lives up to the specificity of its 'scientific' status. When educational researchers or instructors do undertake projects which are not susceptible to 'scientific' treatment (involving a clinical approach, action research, ideological analyses, etc.), the end result is far too often intra-departmental opposition on methodological grounds, or disqualification by those who identify with the norm of traditional university intellectual production.

2. Another confining aspect: university teachers only manage to stabilize their professional status in so far as they achieve recognition as *specialists*. This results in an absence of cooperative teamwork, reinforcing the sectionalization of approaches already inherent in the division of university into 'departments' or 'colleges'. Each academic is obliged to remain within his specific discipline and to speak out, publicly or internationally, only within his own field, to the detriment of an interdisciplinary approach which, and only which, would allow him to seize the entirety of the dimensions of social problems such as they appear in reality. No educational situation, for example, can be reduced to a sociological analysis. Nor can any be approached strictly on an experimental basis, without risking the elimination of decisive factors capable of explaining the identified phenomena. One has only to pick a theme such as youth to be convinced of this.

3. Finally, academic production is initially and essentially destined for use by academics, students and by specialists of a precise field. Doctoral thesis subjects remain significant examples of this phenomenon. The candidate writes above all for his jury. And on the other hand, when university researchers intervene in matters pertaining to their chosen ground, make use of the media, take position on a current issue or take the trouble to vulgarize the results of their research, they are still often accused by their peers of superficiality, if not of demagogy.

Again, the field of education suffers particularly the consequences of these norms of production and diffusion of academic knowledge, because it has the responsibility of shaping and inspiring educational action. In this respect it is striking to note that the most popular works in this field these last years were not produced by writers who have university status or comply to the norms of university publication: P. Freire, I. Illich, A. S. Neill, etc.

The university and modes of intellectual production

Consequently, it is fundamental that the university should not limit itself to expanding the circle of its initiates through creating more flexible admissions policies and inventing new pedagogical formulas (credit systems, schedule changes, individual work).

What is really at stake in opening the university is a radical transformation of the modes of intellectual production. Therefore, it is not so much a question of opening the doors to whomever might want to enter, as that of being willing to break open the system by which the learning that characterizes the university is elaborated and diffused. Rather than demanding that anyone who aspires to a university degree possess a store of cumulative knowledge, the university should contribute to the knowledge which the collectivity lacks, in all areas of life where people today feel at a loss because they no longer know either what to be or what to do. It is time to relinquish the myth of the democratization of university education in order to focus on the role that the university must play in creating *democratic knowledge*. The problem of opening the university then becomes the problem of the public or private character of the knowledge which the university holds in its possession.

This body of knowledge would no longer be the sole property of specialists, but one which academics, by virtue of their specialized competencies, would build with others.[4] Whatever problems one is to consider (education, health, urbanism, collective management and participation, the mechanisms of the economic crisis, or the dangers of environmental pollution), if the university does not assume its role in the creation of knowledge that significantly relates to the crucial problems of contemporary society, it no longer has any reason to exist.

It is not at all a question here of cutting back research budgets or of denying the importance of theoretical conceptualization or of scientific discoveries; it is principally a question of reorienting the ends to which they are used. The isolation of the university is due in large measure to the absence of social agents capable of bridging the gap between work that is properly scientific and the needs of the collectivity. In many disciplines, and notably in the human sciences, only constant interaction between research and teaching, and the concrete questions arising out of adults' social and professional experiences can reduce the chasm between knowledge typically produced at the university and the knowledge necessary to the welfare of society.

The illusion of the transference of knowledge

It is important at this point to insist on our conviction that, despite teachers' claims, their lectures or seminars have only a modest effect on the total learning experience of the students and even less on that of the adults who attend the university. The smattering of ideas memorized and accumulated has only limited impact on the infinitely more vast and complex process by which students and adults learn. Their social experience, the sum of events which influence their lives, their personal curiosity in fields of their choice, and their professional life constitute the many privileged moments of learning that accompany and orient their education. Despite all efforts to rationalize education, the total existentially-acquired learning is greater than the restricted body of scientific knowledge transmitted by the university.

The building of knowledge in an experiment in educational self-management

The position taken here is largely the result of the opportunity I had a few years ago to participate in an educational experiment which allowed me to radicalize my criticism of my teaching at the university. A specialized course in community organization was offered to social workers in the French-speaking part of Switzerland. It was organized around a highly-structured programme including both lectures on specific subjects — community sociology, social administration, political economy, etc. — and practical supervisory seminars. A majority of the instructors called upon to train the social workers for collective action were university teachers. These experts were to speak on one aspect of the programme. Each lecturer, in fact, succeeded more or less in communicating the product of his research and personal thinking, depending on whether he was able to interest his listeners or be receptive to their concerns. I was made responsible for the course evaluation. I first of all understood this task with the help of an 'objectives grid' designed to measure the degree of the participants' satisfaction, especially with regard to the relationship they were able to establish between the lectures and their professional practice.

This first systematic evaluation, made after three months of lectures, brought to light a profound split between the underlying aims of the programme and the expectations of the participants. The knowledge dispensed, occasionally recognized as interesting in itself, did not speak to their concerns. The social workers were reluctant to receive specialized knowledge which did not provide them with what they judged to be necessary tools for analysis and action. The sociological, economic and pedagogical information that was presented was felt to distract them from their real preoccupations. Unable to endure this learning situation, they achieved the feat of forcing the resignation of the course leader and of taking over the direction of the course themselves. The director of the Institute responsible for supervising the course, together with the sponsoring committee, agreed to this power transfer, and a contract was drawn up with the participants, which made the latter totally responsible for the course content and the pedagogical methods to be used.

From this time on, the eighteen participants entered into a self-management educational process characterized by constant reflection on the nature of the knowledge pertinent to their training. Disagreements were frequent within the group. Discussions dealing with the participants' expectations brought out the points of divergency in their thinking, as well as contradictory styles of practice. Given the work pace (one entire work-week each month), it took more than a year for the group to discover little by little that the knowledge pertinent to community organization was inseparable from the reflection that each person could contribute by draw-ing from his professional life and social involvements, as well as from the group's constant analysis of its functional difficulties. Progressively, group members ceased thinking that the only knowledge worthy of attention was that of outside speakers. They gradually came to understand that the recognition of their own knowledge was the necessary condition for the broadening of their learning in the areas under study. After that, they con-structed their programme in relation to questions arising from their own practical experience. And finally, they understood that the body of know-ledge they really needed had to be put together with the help of diverse resources: lectures by specialists, meeting with experts or people respon-sible for significant community experiments, discussion minutes, sys-tematic presentations of their respective experiences in community organization, etc. The final group evaluation clearly showed how much of what they learned in the course contributed to their overall development.

Applications of this experiment to adult education

This experiment appears exemplary. It denounces the illusions of university-transmitted knowledge (however interesting the latter, on the theoretical level), which fails to take into account the questions, and more generally the characteristics, of the adults for whom it is destined.

The experiment indicates that only that knowledge which intervenes as a *regulator* of professional, personal or social activity can really be assimi-lated. It shows that for a group of adults trying to specialize profession-ally, a programme is only formative in so far as each of its members examines critically his past schooling and attempts to define his relation-ship to knowledge. It demonstrates that adults only become the authors of their gradually-acquired knowledge when they are given the possibility of directing their own *education* and consequently, of becoming the actors in a programme of courses and the agents of their own learning process. The group's publication of a book[5] (which retraces the principal stages of its progress) shows that it recognized itself publicly capable of com-municating to others the knowledge which it had itself produced.

The opening of academic knowledge

This experiment took place outside the university but within the frame-work of an institution of higher education. The autonomy which the latter institute enjoys is certainly not irrelevant to the direction which the course took. It is, however, not inconceivable that the university plays a role in imagining and promoting such experiments. What is significant here, is that the learning process took place independently of the norms traditionally imposed by university programmes. This makes me resolute in the conviction that the central issues involved in the question of the democratization of knowledge and in the dialogue between theory-building and practical, social experience, will not be essentially resolved by opening university programmes to more people, but rather by creating interaction between the scientific or theoretical knowledge emanating from the university and the questions being formulated in different institutions of adult education. In other words, the presence of teachers and researchers outside academic walls, in areas of professional and cultural experimentation which analysis of political forces and of the most urgent social problems would show to be priority, seems to me to be today the primary condition for a real broadening of academic knowledge. The opening of academic knowledge would become a valid alternative to the opening of the university's structure.

If this alternative were carried out, a certain number of practical changes would take place. To allow teachers to redistribute their work loads and devote sufficient time to outside consultations, the responsibilities and schedule would have to be modified, thereby changing both the nature of academic competency and criteria for appointments. Outside involvements would no longer be considered 'extra', but would become the activity that would make teaching and research significant.

Theoretical requirements and the quality of critical, creative reflection would not be reduced, but academic work would be reoriented to focus on the concrete problems under debate in social groups, however diverse and marginal (socio-cultural work groups, the media, medicine, community organization, for example).

In this perspective, the university must avoid limiting its effort to that of favouring individual mobility through the giving of preferential treatment to adults whose incomplete schooling handicaps their professional ambitions.

It is essential that the university give priority to those who, in the light of their responsibilities (in administration, labour unions, training centres, for example), can become the promoters of a collective type of training which would draw together all concerned adults.

The time has come to go beyond the mere certification of accumulated knowledge. It is time to bring forth tangible signs of an open knowledge which would represent the presence of a variety of university publics; this public would be composed of diverse social actors who, through *successive self-regulations*, would return to the university from time to time, according to need. As a result of this 'coming and going' of a continuous but diversified public at the university, this 'new knowledge' could be constructed in direct contact with social reality, in the social, political and professional meeting places of the various 'social actors'.[6] To accomplish this it is indispensable that new organizational ways and means be found to join university research and teaching with all retraining or continuous education activities coming under the general heading of adult education.

Likewise, just as one should think in terms of learning process rather than years of study, the knowledge necessary to adults throughout their lives must be understood in terms of its various dimensions as it is acquired within the complex network of formal and informal educational activities.

Toward new strategic options

The alternative to present policies concerning the opening of the university presented here does not postulate its adoption tomorrow. My intention is rather to underline that in our society, the strategic importance of educational experiments is more promising than the compromises characteristic of legislative reform. The more the university considers the role it should play in continuous adult education, the more it, and all other institutions of higher education, will have to redefine priorities.

Throughout this chapter, I have tried to show that the primary issue at stake in this debate centres around the concept of knowledge maintained by the university. In proposing not an increase in the number of students, but a change in the conditions in which knowledge may be produced, I have opted for a strategic orientation which goes against the current of certain efforts made the last few years. I am perfectly conscious of the fact. But I believe that instead of nurturing intellectual or cultural privileges by trying to enlarge the circle of the elite, it is preferable that those teachers who wish to change the university begin by tackling the critical problems of contemporary civilization and by contributing, given their specialized competencies and with the help of increased collaboration, to the conception and invention of solutions to these problems.

It is partly in this direction that my colleagues and I seek to orient the development of our sector of adult education. Through the educational projects to which we have given priority — whether in the areas of training women, trade union leaders or health personnel — we are trying, with a restricted and representative population of what I have named social actors, to discover 'half-way' between the university and the city, strategic lines and operational means for *real* adult education — an education that is neither a type of cultural colonization nor a simple adjusting of work qualifications recently required on the job market — an education based on the collective creation of the kind of knowledge that can transform life conditions, professional experience or cultural life. The future will reveal whether this type of experimentation will lead the university to new horizons and — when political change gives such experiences recognition — actually become real alternatives.

The editors wish to thank R. Pfitzer and E. Dominicé for translating this chapter.

References

1. M. Carton, 'Le Centre Universitaire de Roskilde: une interprétation socio-économique d'une innovation au Danemark', Genève, Bureau International de l'Education, *Expériences et Innovations en Education* (1976), 29.
2. For a real innovation see: J. Debelle, P. Demunter and I. Hecquet, 'Une Université ouverte à Charleroi, Etude de la Fondation Européenne de la Culture', *JEB* 1/1975.
3. F. Edding, 'Les conditions de l'éducation récurrente au niveau supérieur', Strasbourg, Conseil de l'Europe, Document AS/Cult. (24), 10 révisé, 1972.
4. 'The object of the research process, like the object of the educational process, should be the liberation of human creative potential and the mobilization of human resources for the solution of social problems' in B. Hall, 'Participatory Research: An Approach for Change', *Convergence* II/1975.
5. Ouvrage collectif, *Le développement communautaire ou les contradictions du travail social*, Genève, CSESS, 1975.
6. Cf. G. Daoust et P. Bélanger, *L'Université dans une société éducative. De l'éducation des adultes à l'éducation permanente.* Montréal, Les Presses de l'Université de Montréal, 1974.

Chapter 3

Higher education alternatives in developing countries

Eric Williams ·

Walt Whitman was once asked: 'What would you say about the University and modern life?' Whitman replied: 'I wouldn't say anything. I'd rather be excused.'

Such poetic licence is for the poet only. A UNESCO Commission, in its report of 1972: *Learning To Be: The World of Education Today and Tomorrow*, warns: 'We may be heading for a veritable dichotomy within the human race, which risks being split into superior and inferior groups, into masters and slaves, supermen and submen.'

There is no 'may be' about it. The dichotomy is here, right now, and it has always been here. It is here in the comparison between the developed and the developing countries.

From 1960 to 1968, public expenditure on education in the world rose from $54,400 million to $132,000 million, an increase of nearly 150 per cent. Education expenditure as a percentage of Gross National Product rose, for the world as a whole, from 3 per cent in 1960 to 4¼ per cent in 1968. Specific increases in respect of the percentage of State budgets allocated to education in different regions of the world are as follows:

North America	from 15.6 to 17 per cent
Europe	from 13.5 to 15 per cent
Asia	from 11.8 to 13.2 per cent
Latin America	from 12.6 to 15.4 per cent
Africa	from 14.5 to 16.4 per cent
Oceania	from 10.4 to 15.7 per cent
World expenditure	from 13.5 to 15.5 per cent

These increases in expenditure represented a corresponding increase in the percentage of Gross National Product allocated to education in both groups of countries as follows:

Developed countries	from 3.52 to 4.80 per cent of GNP, which increased by 78 per cent
Developing countries	from 2.73 to 3.91 per cent of GNP, which increased by 62 per cent

The dichotomy lies in the Gross National Product (GNP) itself, as the following summary comparing developed and developing countries ten years ago demonstrates:

1. Thirty-one developing countries with a GNP of less than $100 had a combined average GNP of $2,245, less than Switzerland. The developing countries included 23 in Africa and 6 in Asia; 2 were OPEC countries (Indonesia and Nigeria); one was a Latin American country, Haiti.
2. Twenty-two developing countries, with a per capita GNP between $100 and $200, had a combined average GNP of $3,048, less than Australia and New Zealand combined. The developing countries included 9 in Africa, 10 in Asia, 1 in Latin America.
3. Twenty-three developing countries, with a per capita GNP between $200 and $300, had a combined average GNP of $5,598, less than USA and Canada combined. The developing countries included 8 in Africa, 7 in Latin America, 5 in the Middle East, 5 OPEC countries (Gabon, Iraq, Iran, Saudi Arabia, Algeria).
4. Seventeen countries, with a per capita GNP between $300 and $400, had a combined average GNP of $6,790, less than Scandinavia — Norway, Sweden, Denmark. These countries included 10 developing countries in Latin America as well as Yugoslavia and Portugal in Europe.
5. Six developing countries, with a per capita GNP between $500 and $600, had a combined GNP of $3,243, less than West and East Germany combined. One of these countries was an OPEC country, Libya; 1 was a European country, Spain; 2 were Latin American.

Thus it was that in 1968 the developed industrialized countries, with one-third of the world's population, one-quarter of the world's young people, spent ten times more money on education than the developing countries — $120,000 million as against $12,000 million. The UNESCO Commission itself reported in 1972 that for every five students in the European and North American higher educational systems there were two in all the other regions of the world combined. Specific ratios are:

North America	1 : 8
Europe	1 : 20
Asia	1 : 38
Arab States	1 : 45
Latin America	1 : 49
Africa	1 : 90

The dichotomy, there's the enemy! And the alternative for the developing countries? To catch up with the developed countries is out of the question. Either increase the GNP — academic in these days of inflation — or concentrate on the priorities in the educational infrastructure. As the report of the UNESCO Commission, 1972, states:

But given the fact that State educational expenditure is increasing from year to year, we must decide what proportion of the additional increment should be used to develop and perfect formal school establishments and what amounts should be allocated to other needs, especially to Adult

*Education, pre-school education and the development of educational tech-
nology. It is here in particular that the developing countries must work out
their own destiny.*

The first such area is literacy. The world illiteracy rate among adults
over 15 is as follows:

Year	Number (millions)	% of total world population
1950	700	44.3
1960	735	39.3
1970	783	34.2
1980 (est.)	820	29

The position in the major regions of the world was as follows in 1970:

	%	Number (millions)
North America	1.5	
Europe	3.6	
Latin America	23.6	40
Asia	46.8	+500
Arab countries	73.0	50
Africa	73.7	145

The regional imbalance is further aggravated by the sexual imbalance. The
African illiteracy rate breaks down into 63.4 per cent male and 83.7 per
cent female; a similar disproportion exists in the Arab countries, with 60.5
per cent of men and 85.7 per cent of women illiterate.

The gravity and urgency of the problem of illiteracy were emphasized
when UNESCO in 1965 convened a world congress of Ministers of Education at Teheran to consider in general what action should be taken to deal
with illiteracy. Out of the Teheran Conference emerged a new concept of
'functional literacy', and during 1973 an experimental programme, sup-
ported by international assistance, was being implemented in sixteen
Africa, Latin American and Asian countries: Afghanistan, Algeria,
Ecuador, Ethiopia, Guinea, India, Iran, Kenya, Madagascar, Mali, Niger,
Sudan, Syrian Arab Republic, Tanzania, Venezuela, Zambia.

Such countries as the Soviet Union, China, Algeria and Brazil have
tackled the problem of illiteracy on a large scale with some success. The
Cuban effort has attracted much publicity. In 1961 Cuba initiated a
national campaign which utilized 120 volunteers, 105,000 pupils released
from their schools, and 20,000 workers to act as voluntary teachers in the
campaign. The campaign was officially declared over before the year ended
when it was reported that more than 700,000 adults had learned to read
and write and illiteracy had dropped from 23 per cent to less than 4 per
cent.

The conclusion reached by the UNESCO Commission of 1972 is
relevant:

Even in areas where campaigns against illiteracy appear to be producing results, these are frequently of a purely formal nature without any really significant consequences for educational development. All in all, few literacy campaigns have achieved what are generally agreed nowadays to be the real objectives of the struggle against literacy. The aim is not simply to enable an illiterate person to decipher words in a textbook but to become better integrated into his environment, to have a better grasp of real life, to enhance his personal dignity, to have access to sources of knowledge which he personally may find useful, to acquire the know-how and the techniques he needs in order to lead a better life.

A second major problem facing the developing countries, which would inevitably determine the priority to be accorded to higher education expansion, is the large number of children not accommodated within the primary school system, further aggravated by the problems of wastage and drop-outs.

For the past two decades UNESCO has made this question one of its major concerns, in a series of regional meetings. The targets set at these meetings for universal primary education were as follows:

Asia: Karachi   28 Dec. 1959 to   1980 target
                             9 Jan. 1960
Africa: Addis Ababa   15—25 May 1961   1980, with 71 per
                                                    cent in 1970
Latin America: Santiago   5—19 March 1962   1970
Arab States: Tripoli   9—14 April 1966   1980

Have these targets been achieved? If achieved, the dichotomy would be clearly between the higher education of the developed and the primary education of the developing. But they have not been realized, as is indicated below:

	1970 enrolment (%)	1985 projection (%)
Asia	65	67
Africa	44	44
Latin America	92 for temperate region; less than 80 in others	75
Northern Africa (Arab)	52	48

The picture of school enrolment rates that emerged at UNESCO's Venezuela Conference in 1972 was as shown on Table 3.1:

The UNESCO Report of 1972 gave the following details (Table 3.2) — of school enrolment rates from 1967 to 1968 at different levels of education, comparing the major regions of the world:

Table 3.2 indicates that, in respect of developing countries, if less than 5 per cent go on to higher education, and less than 30 per cent go on to

Table 3.1   Percentage of children of school-age

	Primary		Secondary		Primary plus secondary	
	1960	1970	1960	1970	1960	1970
World	63	71	32	54	50	63
Developed countries						
North America	98	99	90	93	94	97
Europe	96	97	57	67	79	85
Developing countries						
Latin America	60	70	21	49	45	65
Asia	50	59	22	44	36	55
Africa	34	48	12	25	24	38
Arab countries	38	61	16	28	28	45

Table 3.2

	Children of primary school-age attending school (at any level)	Children of secondary school-age attending school (at any level)	Students registered for higher education in relation to young people aged 20—24
North America	98	92	44.5
Europe and USSR	97	65	16.7
Oceania	95	60	15.0
Latin America	75	35	5.0
Arab States	(50)	(25)	(3.1)
Asia	55	30	4.7
Africa	40	15	1.3

secondary school, half the total population has never been to school. Between 1960 and 1968, the numbers of children between 5 and 14 who were unable to attend school increased by 17 million; every year 2 million more children were refused the right to an education. In these years the proportion of school-age children attending primary schools rose by not more than 4 percentage points in Africa, 9 points in Asia, and 10 points in Latin America and the Arab countries.

The developed countries have 22 per cent of the world's children under 15 and 25 per cent of the school-age population 5 to 24. The developing countries have 78 per cent of the world's children under 15. But between 1960 and 1968 developed countries had an equal share with the developing countries of the world school enrolments; the increase in secondary and primary school enrolments in developed countries ran parallel to the increase in the number of young people between 5 and 19, while in developing countries the population between 5 and 19 years of age increased by 36 million more than the increase in school enrolment.

As the UNESCO Commission of 1972 stated:

In half of the countries of the world, half the children enrolled in schools fail to complete the primary cycle. Even if we consider only those who leave school after their first, second or third year — that is, for the most part, having acquired little lasting benefit — the fact remains that in many countries the money spent on them absorbs between 20 and 40 per cent of the total State education budget. . . .

For hundreds of millions of illiterate people in the world, school can no longer be of help. In the developing countries, nearly half the children of primary school-age today are condemned, no matter what happens, to grow up without ever having attended a class.

Admittedly this is not a problem of developing countries only. Wastage and drop-outs in Belgium are estimated at 28 per cent for primary education as a whole and in France at 50 per cent for the last two years at the primary level. But the developing countries are hit even harder. In Thailand 17 per cent only survive to class V; it needs 4.7 years of education investment to produce one leaver in class IV, and of these class IV leavers only 57 per cent can be considered fundamentally literate. In Dahomey only one in five entering school reaches his fifth year; in Zaire four out of five children in primary school do not get as far as the primary school-leaving certificate; in one unidentified African country, the unit cost of the primary school certificate is seven times higher than it would be without repetition and drop-outs from classes 1 to 6.

UNESCO figures for out-of-school youth comparing developed and developing regions are as follows (in millions):

	Age 6—11		Age 12—17	
	1960	1970	1960	1970
More developed	11	8	20	16
Less developed	118	113	136	163
South Asia	75	69	87	108
Africa	28	31	29	33
Latin America	14	12	18	19

A third major problem for the developing countries in respect of education at lower levels is the inequality within the countries themselves — the disparity between education in urban areas and education in rural areas. In Dahomey an average school enrolment rate at the primary level is 30 per cent — it is 68 per cent in the capital but only 12 per cent in remote areas. In one country in Latin America 66 per cent of primary schools in urban areas offered the full five years of the elementary education cycle as compared with 6 per cent in rural areas; 59 per cent of village schools provided only two years of schooling. The Colombia experience is instructive:

(a) Out of 1,000 pupils entering primary schools, 507 will reach the fifth class in the urban system, 40 in the rural areas
(b) Ninety-two per cent of rural schools do not give pupils the opportunity of completing a primary education.
(c) This adds up to an illiteracy rate of 10 per cent in Bogota, the capital, compared with 82 per cent in one rural administrative division.

The World Bank has sought to put in a nutshell this dichotomy in education by presenting a hypothetical developing country, Independencia, of 5 million people and a population growth rate of 2.5 per cent per year. These are the vital statistics of Independencia:

School-age population	Primary (6—11) 800,000; secondary (12—17) 650,000; tertiary (18—21) 370,000
School enrolment ratios (per cent)	Primary 50; secondary 10; tertiary 2 (ratios (per cent) are 43, 5, 0.4 for 23 developing countries with 168 million people)
GNP	US $100 per capita (for 29 developing countries in 1973, US $120 or less)
Education finance	4 per cent of GNP, 18 per cent of public revenues (corresponding to 64 countries in 1974)
Ten-year plan	Increase in enrolment: Primary to 90 per cent; secondary to 27 per cent; tertiary to 4.9 per cent
Recurrent costs	1974 — US $22 m.; 1983 — US $122 m. — almost six times as much

Education recurrent costs as per cent of GNP: 1974 — 4; 1983 — 14

The World Bank study concludes:

It is doubtful if other priorities of a developing country such as agriculture, industry, communication, health, will receive enough funds if education receives more than, say, 30% of the public revenues. . . .

The targets suggested in Independencia's 10-year education plan are comparatively modest by standards of the developed countries. There would still remain great gaps and deficiencies in the education system, and a large portion of the population would remain illiterate. . . .

The education plan would place a heavy burden on Independencia's economy despite an increase of the GNP by 76% and of the GNP/capita of 38%. The aggregate recurrent and capital education costs would amount to 15% of the GNP and to 62% of the public revenues at the end of the period. The latter percentage assumes that 24% of GNP would continue to be public revenues. It is not economically feasible, and politically possible to give such a high priority to education in any country, be it rich or poor . . . few of the poorest developing countries can afford to expand or improve their education system along the traditional lines.

The World Bank in its recommendations gives priority to the possibility of slowing down the increase in teachers' salaries, pointing out that primary teachers' salaries are two to three times as high as the GNP per capita in six developed countries whilst they were four times as high in twenty-four developing countries, varying from two to eighteen times. As other means of reducing costs, the World Bank suggested refraining from decreases in class sizes and from increases in teacher qualifications.

Such proposals are bound to be unpopular and to be resisted, especially in the context of increasing unionization of the teaching profession. Against this must be placed the recognition by education authorities in Zambia that in the rush to expand education following independence in 1964, 'we opened more schools than we could look after', and in Malaysia that the quality of secondary education declined following the abolition of the secondary school entrance examination as a result of a crash building programme, increases in class size, and recruitment of unqualified teachers given training on weekends and holidays.

Much talk has developed in respect of other possibilities, principally educational technology. India has blazed the trail in the use of satellites to relay rural education programmes. In Ivory Coast the greater part of primary education is televised; a five-year plan calls for 16,500 classes equipped with TV by 1980, to cater to first grade classes, youths between 13 and 17, and the entire adult population for cultural activities. By 1986 it is envisaged that the total 6 to 11 age-group will be enrolled and receiving televised education. The World Bank stresses that the annual recurrent cost per student in Ivory Coast televised education was $115 for 21,000 students and $6 for 700,000 students; and that the cost of maintaining the traditional system would cost the country 44 per cent more than TV education. But warning notes have been sounded in developing countries.

(a) At the UNESCO Conference on Adult Education in Tokyo, face to face with the aggressiveness of the adult educators' lobby in developed countries, the developing world was somewhat taken aback by the scale of dissent and the criticism of the 'increasingly anomalous and paralysing perpetuation of an education system which alone swallowed up a third of the country's budget'.

(b) The developing world regarded the emphasis on educational technology and particularly the mass media as something of more concern to the developed world with its sophisticated technology. What if everybody had a transistor radio but there was no message of any importance to receive! In the words of the report on the Tokyo Conference particularly with reference to Third World countries, 'several delegates voiced concern about the present use of the mass media especially television. There was a mystique in certain countries about television that had to be resisted'. Principally from Latin America came criticisms of the excessive investments, the unsuitability of imported programmes, and the high pressure publicity methods, as well as the criticism of the mass media as too authoritarian since they did not allow for feed back.

(c) The report of the UNESCO Commission of 1972, proposing universal principles for the education of tomorrow, is regarded in many Third World countries as 'confusing the modernization of education systems with recourse to Western technologies'.

The developing countries are in no position to consider, as one of the alternatives facing them in the development of their higher education systems, that they should concentrate on catching up with the developed countries. The dichotomy is there and will remain there as Table 3.3, showing expenditure per head of the school-age population 5 to 19 in selected countries indicates:

Table 3.3

Country	Year	Expenditure ($)
USA	1967	771
West Germany	1967	375
France	1967	341
Australia	1967	321
Italy	1967	296
Japan	1967	187
Venezuela	1967	98
Chile	1966	69
Iraq	1966	41
Algeria	1967	39
Ghana	1965	35
UAR	1967	23
Taiwan	1967	22
Sri Lanka	1966	18
Colombia	1966	17
Philippines	1967	14
Kenya	1965	12
Thailand	1966	11
India	1965	8
Brazil	1966	7
Nigeria	1965	5
Pakistan	1967	4
Ethiopia	1967	2

The expenditure in the USA alone exceeded the combined expenditure of seventeen developing countries (three of them OPEC countries). Japan spends eleven times as much per head as Colombia, twenty-three times as much as India — yet West Germany spends twice as much as Japan and the USA more than four times as much.

Consider the grim reality of the dichotomy in Pakistan. In West Pakistan (before the partition of the country) the cost of primary education per child per annum in 1965 was 90 cents — less than 5 cents of which represented paper, equipment, chalk, teaching aids, books. The equivalent cost of such supplies in a typical American suburban school was $30 — 600 times as much. Things were even worse in East Pakistan.

The emulation of the universities of developed countries as a possible alternative for the developing countries will bring the latter into contact with the student dissent of the decades of the 'sixties and the experimentation now under way at the level of university administration, in respect of student criticisms regarding restructuring the universities and making the curriculum more relevant to the needs of the age.

The student dissent of the 'sixties raged like a bush fire through the higher education system in the developed countries. This was not only a matter of American universities though perhaps they made the most noise. It involved other developed countries as well, and whilst there was Berkeley, Columbia, Cornell, there were also the London School of Economics, the Sorbonne, Amsterdam, Berlin, Tokyo and Toronto. It seems to have been sudden and to have taken people by surprise; certainly in Berkeley at the beginning of the free speech movement in 1964 a routine sociological survey showed that 80 per cent of the students surveyed were satisfied with the university and with the education they had been receiving. The subsidence of the passions aroused seemed to have been equally sudden, and it is commonplace to acknowledge that the university discontent of the 'sixties was only one of a number of other social problems international in scope: urban blight, environmental decay, racism, poverty, crime in the streets, the energy crisis.

This may well be true, but it would be a mistake to conclude that all is over, that God's still in his heaven (though so many say He is dead), and all's well with the world. A recent Gallup poll suggests that two out of five students continue to believe in the efficacy of violence, and that concern over political morality has replaced the anger over the Vietnam War. We recall that the Students for a Democratic Society had emphasized in 1965 that students saw America's problems 'not in Vietnam or China or Brazil or outer space or at the bottom of the ocean but here in the United States'.

But the sudden dissent of the 'sixties has shown us that all the talk of restructuring revolves around a number of fundamental problems in higher education for developed countries which cannot be ignored by developing countries whether they seek to perpetuate their dependence on the developed countries or seek an alternative to it.

The first fundamental issue is the scope of the university and its purpose for the education of young people of a certain age after high school and before they go to work, approximately between the ages of 17 and 24, in an undergraduate college with graduate work and professional preparation superimposed on it. The traditional concept of this system of higher education is that it must be uninterrupted. This was brought into question especially with the Second World War, the interruption of studies and the expansion of the university under State subsidies of veterans who are adults, married and with families, and more positive in their views of their future career than younger undergraduates before the war. The reality behind this is the egalitarian attitude of access to the university and protests against the establishment for the exclusion of large numbers of people whether on class, racial or sexual grounds from a university career.

This at once raises inevitably two burning problems of the present. The first is overproduction of graduates in particular fields, included in this being the idolatry of the PhD. The Bureau of the Census in the USA claims that a college graduate earns $279,000 more than a high school graduate over their lifetimes. If this is so, it must be very disturbing to learn today that there are not enough teaching positions in the US to take care of all the college teachers being turned out by the graduate schools; that 100 faculty members of the State University of Southern Illinois have recently been retrenched partly because the university was unable in 1973 to enrol enough students to utilize the faculty positions authorized; that (according to the US Bureau of Labor Statistics) a majority of the jobs of the future will not require a four-year college education.

The second crucial problem of the day is the tyranny of examinations leading up to what has been called honours inflation and the meaninglessness of many of the different grades awarded to students in universities. US university statistics show graduation with honours by 16 per cent of the class in 1970, 19 per cent in 1971, 23.5 per cent in 1972, 27 per cent in 1973, 42 per cent in 1974. *Cum laude* degrees increased by 255 per cent between 1964 and 1974, *magna cum laude* degrees by 358 per cent, *summa cum laude* degrees by 489 per cent.

A second major slogan in the contemporary dissent is the irrelevance of the curriculum and its inadequacy. Beginning with the original respect to the point of reverence for the ancient classical civilizations of Greece and Rome in Western Europe that had emerged by 1500, the traditional emphasis of Western higher education was classical languages, Latin and Greek, emphasized as the proper training for the man, an inspiration through the character of the societies to the young students of Europe. This basic concern with a prescribed curriculum gave way under the impact of American democracy to the system of student elections, the student having a large say in the choice of subjects for study. This led to inevitable competition among faculties and departments to build up each his own little satrapy, reduce compulsory courses taking the student away from his 'major', and completely losing sight of the old adage that the proper study of mankind is Man by breaking up the body of knowledge into a number of separate and disconnected compartments. As has been said, 'We entered the age of the Green Stamp University, in which the student receives the same number of stamps for a course on Bay Area pollution or human sexuality as he does for American history or the Greek philosophers, sticks them happily into his book, and gets a diploma when it is filled.'

Basic to all this fragmentation has been the supersession of the humanities and especially history by the disciplines of science and technology and the professional schools of medicine, law and engineering. The crux of the dilemma of higher education in developed countries is expressed in that lament at Cornell that it was possible for a student to get a bachelor's degree in arts and science without having been required to read a line of Plato, the Bible, Shakespeare, Marx or Einstein. In the words of one contemporary analyst of the present position in the United States:

Many established colleges . . . have today no requirements at all outside the field of concentration and few within it, except for a course in English composition. It is thus theoretically possible to be graduated without exposure to the historical dimension of existence in any form ... the emancipation of the new college generation from western culture is virtually complete ... the past has become a luxury in our civilisation ... there is a poverty of historical culture in the university.

Add to this what some other critics call the tendency to monolingualism and the elimination of the traditional requirement of a foreign language – down from 89 per cent of US universities and colleges in 1965 to 56 per cent in 1974.

The third major feature of contemporary problems in the university in developed countries relates to the problem of size and the new responsibilities it has undertaken. There is an old-established tradition which continues to emphasize research among the faculty at the expense of teaching. Sooner or later one was bound to arrive at the law of diminishing returns in respect of the adequacy of or improvement on many of the subjects for research in the different disciplines, and sooner or later by tradition possibly the teacher was bound to come back into his own. All this has been aggravated by the active association of universities with the so-called military/industrial establishment and the research related emphatically to the war in Vietnam. Side by side with this has gone not merely the increasing dependence of the universities on the State for its funds, but the obsession of the university with managerial functions related to the size of the establishment and the growth of the non-academic staff with the inevitability of unionization. The university of the developed world has become not only the knowledge factory on which much scorn is poured because of its diversity and fragmentation, but also a huge industry, a huge business enterprise in which talent and qualification no longer matter, or if they do, they have their price.

To such an extent has the pendulum swung in the other direction from universities with their own housing settlements and student residences and golf courses and swimming pools, the Assembly of University Goals and Governance established by the American Academy of Arts and Science in September 1969 has now, in 1975, called on the American university to discontinue much of its non-intellectual and entrepreneurial deviations. The Assembly recommends: 'Private industry or nonprofit corporations ought to be encouraged to supply services now offered by colleges and universities to their students. Considerable savings might be realised by such policies. Also, a more sensitive response to changing student needs might be registered. Housing, dining facilities, career counselling, health, and medical services might be supplied more reasonably by outside agencies.'

Yet another ancient shibboleth has had to bite the dust. For those who traditionally saw the university *in loci parentis* but now have to accommodate themselves to a student dissent calling for co-educational dormitories, the Assembly further recommends: 'on campuses the responsibility for residence halls and other living arrangements ought to rest with students, as is the case in several European countries'.

In addition to these basic organizational problems — the age groups concentrated upon, the curriculum irrelevance and inadequacy, the entrepreneurial functions of the university — there are other fundamental aspects of the contemporary university in developed countries which have great significance for developing countries today considering possible higher education alternatives.

In the first place higher education in developed countries was exclusive in scope and limited to privileged classes.

First and foremost it excluded the working class and it excluded women. In the words of the eighteenth-century Frenchman Linguet, everything would be lost once the workers knew that they had a mind. It was only at the end of the first quarter of the nineteenth century in Britain that a breach in the aristocratic tradition was made with the emergence of London University as a particular area for education of the British middle class.

The situation in France is particularly instructive. Between 1962 and 1966, the rate of objective probability of access to higher education rose as follows: farm workers, from 1.1 to 2.7; farmers, from 3.4 to 8; workers from 1.3 to 3.4; white-collar workers, from 9 to 16.2. Compare the children from more favoured social and employment categories: industrialists, from 54.4 to 71.5; middle-grade personnel, from 24.9 to 35.4; professionals and higher executives, from 38 to 58.7. The lack of balance had become worse. France is no exception to the general rule of developed countries. Great Britain shows a similar imbalance in the same years — 4 per cent of the children of skilled and 2 per cent of those of semi-skilled and unskilled workers. The children of these two groups form only 30 per cent of the student population in Great Britain, 12.6 per cent in France, 11.5 per cent in Belgium, 10 per cent in the Netherlands, 7.5 per cent in West Germany.

Distribution of State grants does little to relieve the imbalance or to make up for variations in resources of the different social groups. France is a good example. In 1968—69 the percentage distribution per 100 higher education grants was as follows: farmers, 11.2; industrial and business leaders, 9.6; liberal professions and senior employees, 6.3; middle-grade personnel, 12; white-collar workers, 12.2; industrial workers, 22.2; farm workers, 2.1; employees in service industries, 2.2; retired individuals, 8.5; miscellaneous, 13.7. In the words of a UNESCO study on the democratization of higher education: 'It is obvious that scales for awards which, per 100 grants, give only 12 to children of white-collar workers, 22 to children of industrial workers but almost 16 to children of the owners of businesses and higher executives are not completely democratic, do not equalize poverty itself, and perpetuate a regrettable social discrimination.'

It is in democratic Sweden, on all counts leader in the area of access to education, that one can see what still remains to be done. The percentage intake of children into the gymnasia (comprehensive schools) from the various social groups was: academicians, business executives, higher officials: 72; farmers, primary school teachers, tradesmen, craftsmen: 44; workers in general: 28.

As far as the education of women was concerned, the American egalitarian tradition quite early developed the system of co-education and women's colleges. But it is now fully appreciated that, in the words of one well-known female educator, 'the goal of educating women was the utilitarian one of securing a pool of trained teachers to staff the school system at a minimum of cost'. The experiment began with one of the evangelical colleges, Oberlin. And in the second place, when the question of greater accommodation of women in the higher education system arose, the solution of the problem of women graduates in the sciences and avoiding their competition with men students was resolved by virtually relegating women to the fields of household science and food chemistry instead of the petroleum industry, and advising them to give preference to nursing over medicine.

Women are still trained to be wife and mother and homemaker at the very time when the traditional family is being broken up and maternity and child rearing have become a small part of the woman's life. As one woman sociologist has computed:

For a woman who marries at twenty-two, who works outside the home for three years after marriage and then has two children two years part, and who dies at seventy-four: 23 per cent of her adulthood will be spent without a husband; 41 per cent of her adult life will be spent with a husband but no children under eighteen; 36 per cent of her adulthood will be spent with a spouse and at least one child under eighteen years. So, only 12 per cent of her life will be spent in full-time maternal care of pre-school-age children. Only seven of her fifty-six years will go to pre-school child care.

The second area of exclusiveness in the higher education system in developed countries was the total and uncompromising rejection of the so-called inferior races. The customary alibi is slavery. This is sheer nonsense; slavery in Greece, on which so much of Greek intellectual achievement has been based, was related to virtual monopolies by the slaves of the teaching profession, accounts and clerical work, responsibility for court records, and the virtual restriction of the police force to slaves. The slave systems developed by the developed countries in the New World and elsewhere were fundamentally racist in character. Spanish missionaries found great difficulty in securing approval of the education of Amerindians even when restricted to the purely limited function of participating in church services; and the State in Latin America, whether colonial or independent, applied the strictest regulations regarding so-called purity of blood to admissions to the universities and to the appointment of university teachers. In the Caribbean, the French led the way in their racist obsessions and in the prohibition of education to non-whites and people with any admixture however small of black blood; one of the most infamous decrees of the *ancien régime* stated that it was indecent to see blacks studying to become lawyers. In the early years of Trinidad history as a British colony, one of the serious problems posed for the colonial administration which was referred to the British Government for determination was whether permission should be given to a young man of colour who had returned from England, one Dr Williams, to practise his profession of medicine.

In the third place, university higher education in developed countries was unanimous in its total and unqualified rejection of any studies relating to peoples who did not belong to the white race. The universities were, have been, and in many respects still are, the champions of racial intolerance and intellectual apartheid. It was the British universities in particular which developed the conscious theory and clearly enunciated the pernicious doctrine of the uncivilized Third World and the congenital incapacity of its inhabitants to become civilized. It was the British philosopher of the eighteenth century David Hume, who pontificated that, among African countries and people of African origin, there was no art, no science, no ingenious manufactures.

Thomas Jefferson picked up the theme in the United States of America and went further in depreciating the black man as against the Amerindian; the man who inspired the construction of the University of Virginia, who was so emphatic that the opinion of a ploughman was superior to that of a university professor on moral issues, who so forthrightly trumpeted the inalienable rights of man and the equality of man, made it clear that all of this did not apply to black men and that the black man was mentally unqualified to be exposed to higher education.

It is less than 100 years ago that the *Encyclopaedia Britannica* was denying, at the very time the Europeans were penetrating Africa, that any black man had made any contribution to civilization. The Western university moved steadily with the racial doctrines of Gobineau in France, of Lord Acton with his *Cambridge Modern History* in England and his division of the world into active and passive races, with Madison Grant in America and his lament on the passing of the great race, to the absurdities of the Professor of Modern History at Oxford, Trevor-Roper — that the history of Africa is 'only the unrewarding gyrations of barbarous tribes in picturesque but irrelevant corners of the globe'.

The blacks were not the only victims. It was the higher education of developed countries that in Granada in Spain burned the treasures of Jewish and Muslim manuscripts when the Muslims were thrown out of their last European stronghold; and followed this up in Mexico with the destruction of the invaluable Aztec treasures and manuscripts when Cortes and his band of ruffians overthrew the Aztec empire. Voltaire had to castigate the clergyman Bossuet for daring to write a so-called universal history dealing simply with Jews and Christians, without so much as a mention of Chinese civilization. Walt Whitman with his 'Salut au Monde' was a discordant voice in the intellectual paeans of the western world reflected in Ralph Waldo Emerson's anti-Chinese obscenities, Tennyson's 'Better fifty years of Europe than a cycle of Cathay' and Rudyard Kipling's 'your sullen people half devil and half child'.

The intellectual revolt against this university policy — in the famous words of Edmund Burke, of drawing up an indictment against a whole people — was the black revolt on the campuses in the period of campus dissent and the demand for black studies programmes more relevant to the black historical experience and the black ghetto. The fundamental problem was stated long ago by the grand old man of American history and sociology and the intellectual spokesman of American blacks, W. E. B. Dubois: 'one feels his twoness, an American, a Negro, two souls, two thoughts, two unrecognized strivings, two warring ideals in one dark body, whose dogged strength alone keeps it from being torn asunder'. The few blacks on white campuses found themselves facing 'the white establishment, the white curriculum, the white social environment, the white cultural standards, plus the discovery of apartheid, misunderstanding and experience in the other world in which they found themselves'. They demanded the elimination of institutional racism, the recruitment of more black students and black faculties, the need for black studies programmes and separate facilities for living and cultural and social affairs. Black students on black campuses had never faced any problem of black studies. The black experience had been from the start part of their philosophy and extra-curricular activities. But the tendency of apartheid to breed apartheid was reflected in the growth of the radical black separatist movement aspiring to transform the black colleges into a training ground for building a separatist society; they should have all black students, all black faculties and all black trustees, and use all black money.

The white universities rushed to make compromises and to institute special projects, most of them inferior in quality, and to introduce black personnel specially appointed to teach the special courses — as if the black studies was a curriculum about blacks by blacks and for blacks, as if it were not the white community that needed the black studies. Many of the changes instituted in respect of the black studies programme, as was perhaps inevitable, have survived only where they have been deliberately incorporated with other studies and other disciplines such as economics, history, politics, art or music; one of the outstanding results of the black dissent has been that special fund for the training of black lawyers on condition that after their training they would serve in some parts of the Southern States.

It is in this context that we must view the developments in developed countries, and especially in the United States of America, to deal with the university dissatisfaction related to enrolment, age-groups recruited and curriculum in recent years. From the pioneer Student Experimental College at San Francisco State College developed a host of free universities based on one principle — any one could teach anything he wanted, students could learn or not as they pleased. The free university ran courses from Vietnam and science to black history, experiences in meditation, bicycle trips into the country, organic gardening, readings on Marx and

McLuhan. The free university was a jolting indictment of traditional higher education producing such innovations as the University of Man at Kansas State University which has survived the dissent and enrolls 1,000 students a semester, and the Mid-Peninsula Free University which broke with Stanford University and has become a community night school for the urban counter-culture. Schools experimented with action curricula, such as practical problems of pollution. The pass/fail option was instituted on many campuses in revolt against the archaic grading policy. A new term was experimented with in January between the two traditional semesters, the free term providing an opportunity for all students to win credit for self-initiated or individualized learning. A bewildering proliferation of new institutions and new techniques has emerged, university without walls, open air universities, short cycle education, use of parents as teachers' aides, weekend university, and a whole emphasis on adult education defined as continuing and lifelong education. There have even been developed special courses for prisoners at university level.

A second area of innovation is the policy of open admissions, especially in urban public universities; the policy has been explained as 'to redefine traditional concepts of "the educable" by reaching out to all groups in the metropolitan area, including the academically unprepared'. The policy has been most conspicuously developed at City University of New York, transforming an institution traditionally white and Jewish into a microcosm of New York City's ethnic, racial, and religious distribution — blacks, Puerto Ricans, Irish, Italians. About half the entering freshmen are academically unprepared; of those who entered in September 1970, two out of five were still enrolled by the spring of 1974. The policy has become, it has been said, 'a ticket — for the successful student — out of the ghetto, out of inequality, out of a truncated future'. The price paid by the university is that it has taken on, by its remedial courses for such students, a responsibility that rightfully belongs to the secondary schools. Some universities have accordingly begun to sponsor secondary schools.

A third problem area is the expansion of the sciences. Theodore Roszak, in his campus best seller, *The Making of a Counter Culture*, argues that antipathy to science, as such, rather than simply to the consequences of technology, is the underlying motif of the whole youth protest movement of our time. The villain of the piece, however, is no longer physics, but biology, dramatically different from biology before the Second World War. The enormous development in the fields of genetic medicine and genetic engineering raises fundamental questions of social ethics and individual rights. Society interferes today to require tests for venereal disease as a condition of marriage; does society have any right to dictate genetic testing and counselling for those about to marry? Society today rejects laws forbidding the use of contraceptives by married people; does society have any right to impose compulsory sterilization on individuals, even if a habitual criminal or mentally retarded? As someone has asked of the scientist's power to remove the emotion of rage, the seat of aggression and reduce anxiety or depression, 'would one try to eradicate Faust's restlessness, Hamlet's indecision, King Lear's conscience, Romeo and Juliet's conflicts?' Will society tolerate 'cloning' — the duplication of ourselves, the 'xeroxing of people' as someone has called it?

But we no longer live in an age when scientists are free to do what they want on the ground that the fruits of research are the benefits to society. More and more we face the growing public demand for a more extensive regulation of research — whether nuclear reactors, pesticides and food additives, or new weapons of war. An outstanding example was the public debate in Cambridge, Massachusetts, in January 1977. It related to the new genetic technology, with particular reference to the ability to move genes from one organism to another. Certain Federal guidelines were laid down in 1976 to guard against possible harmful effects and the fear that the new techniques might cause more disease than they cure or might be used to alter human genes. But a group of dissident scientists, taking the view that the guidelines were much too lax and that the research in some cases was too dangerous to do at all, decided to take their case to the public and solicited the support of the Mayor of Cambridge, who had already taken the initiative to plan a public hearing. The dispute involved the biological faculties of Harvard and Massachusetts Institute of Technology and was referred to a review board of Cambridge residents not related to the universities and without expertise in modern biology. The board reported in favour of the guidelines, somewhat modified, developed by the National Institutes of Health, after a sophisticated analysis of the arguments from both sides. Subsequent legislation by the city council established a Cambridge biohazards committee to oversee genetic research done within the city limits.

The mood of the moment in developed countries, where higher education is concerned, is 'lifelong education'; free access of adults to university training whatever the age, whatever the schedule of study, whatever the venue of teaching. Adult education has had a long, respectable and ineffective history over the years, marked by certain principal characteristics:

1. 'pervaded by an atmosphere of amateurism, of mere diversion, cultural chit-chat and therapeutic sociability', to quote a study on European adult education;
2. 'far from being a status symbol of effective living, attendance at adult education courses sometimes and in some of its reaches carried the stigma of participation in something designed for the unsuccessful, the unfortunate, those who have "missed the boat", and those who try to compensate for otherwise dreary and empty lives', to quote again from the Council of Europe study;
3. becomes more urgent when the gap between school-leaving and entry into the labour market has widened, to the disadvantage of those gainfully employed persons in the higher age brackets. In 1910 entrants from school to the labour market in Norway had eight years of schooling, and in 1970 eleven and a half. The Swedish Minister of Education

in 1970 claimed that more than half of those gainfully employed had only six to seven years of schooling;

4. reflected the class nature of the education system. Data from the extramural department of the University of London showed that 56 per cent of the students were in the professional and managerial categories, 20 per cent in the clerical, while 5 per cent were skilled workers and 1 per cent semi-skilled;

5. workers tended to view with suspicion such aspects of the education system as appreciation of music and literature and foreign languages. Studies have demonstrated 'an involuntary rejection of a wide range of valuable experience that restricts the possibilities of personal development for millions of people'. The 'pseudo-culture' of today and the snob interests of so much of what passes for adult education includes the aversion of working-class areas to classical music or to library collections. But Fiat workers in Italy have recently demanded revision of their work schedules to enable them to take advantage of cultural leisure opportunities.

The former Prime Minister of Sweden, Olaf Palme, predicted that the 'seventies will be the decade of adult education. A recent series of projections related to the education of adults with particular reference to Europe can be summarized as follows:

It forecasts a disappearance of the assumption that education is to be equated with youth and associated with establishments such as schools, colleges, and centres. The children of tomorrow will be conditioned to the view that most of their education will come in adult life and will be something to be experienced individually with the potent aid of mechanical apparatus for individual use. A growth in the specialist knowledge related to the type of learning will accelerate the process of transition. The present Swedish tendency to direct the main weight of adult education to bread and butter goals will become general everywhere. The age at which children are regarded as biologically and socially mature will continue to fall. Pluralism of values will intensify to the point of strife, and urban violence will increase.

The dimensions of adult education are being expanded in the context of the following developments:

1. The growth of leisure: it has been estimated that since 1870 the European industrial worker has gained some 1,500 hours a year of leisure in respect of time not devoted to bread winning, to say nothing of earlier pensioned retirement. It is true that as against this, one had to offset the increased prevalence of overtime and moonlighting on the one hand and the greater time lost in travel to work especially in the context of urban relocation and suburban migration. The enhanced importance of leisure is reflected in the increasing use of 'leisure counsellors' by business interests at strategic sites. More significantly, with the growth of unemployment and redundancy of workers — with the lugubrious predictions of sharply decreasing proportions of

graduates and technologists finding employment related to their qualifications, and estimates of 20 per cent of workers becoming unassimi-
lable in industry — the European thinking has already moved in the
direction of opposing any equation of unemployment with poverty or
low social or moral status, and propagating the reorientation of ideas to
the effect that 'unemployment, on adequate pay, is leisure'.

2. Urban renewal and relocation, combined with resiting of industry and
   redeployment of labour, disrupt the traditional slum community with
   its personal relationships.

3. Television, whatever its disruption of family life, has increasingly
   provided the materials of a common culture, making possible discussion
   of the same programmes by peoples in all walks of life.

4. The demand is increasing for the extension of adult education to vocational and bread-and-butter studies as well as liberal and recreational
   studies, in a drive towards qualification for higher earning capacity.
   Contrary to the student dissent, this drive is accompanied by a major
   swing in public opinion and in educational circles generally in favour of
   examinations. The new view is that all people do not need to go to a
   liberal arts college. In the USSR and Poland Workers' Schools train 51
   per cent of skilled workers, 40 per cent of middle-grade technical personnel, and 35 per cent of top-level personnel. The role of the workers'
   universities in Yugoslavia is well known; the forty developed since
   1952, run by workers themselves with a curriculum devoted to productivity and life, enrol 300,000 students. An increase in vocational
   emphasis has been noted in the spread of the gymnasium courses in
   Sweden, where the Labour Market Board provides adult education for
   over 100,000 people each year.

5. To an increasing extent Governments have provided substantial funds
   for adult education. One State in West Germany increased its subventions from half a million marks in 1957 to over 4 million in 1970. If
   workers pay in fees substantial portions of the cost of their universities
   in Yugoslavia, in Ireland a tripartite basis of finances has been worked
   out, the taxpayer financing half the cost. The Scandinavian scheme for
   loan funds to students whatever the age, with generous conditions for
   repayment, is perhaps the decisive example in the contemporary world
   of guaranteeing equal access to education, motivated no doubt by the
   report of its Low Income Committee in 1970 that workers with a
   secondary school education receive a wage much higher than those with
   only a primary school education amounting to 36 per cent in the age-
   group 14—24, 55 per cent in the age-group 25—34, 88 per cent in the
   age-group 35—44, and 127 per cent in the age-group 45—64.

6. From 1969 in Sweden all those over 25 who have had five years' experience of work may be admitted to universities even though they lack
   those certificates which are normally gained through prolonged secondary education. In Norway it has been proposed that adult education
   should be made compulsory. Beginning with West Germany, there is
   discussion of the possibility of paid release from work to education

during ten days in the year for all workers. This has become the National Agreement of July 1970 in France between the Federation of Employers and the Confederation of Trade Unions.

Much of this ferment stems from the new values being agitated everywhere. To give some examples:

(a) Proposals for a new school day propose a division into three equal time segments — (i) learning fundamental skills and areas of knowledge, thus challenging the basis of the traditional curriculum; (ii) a period open for the students to choose any area they want to learn more about; (iii) education of the self.

(b) 'The nuclear family is a nuclear disaster.' The traditional family portrayed in school books, a 'normal' two-parent home with a dominant working father and a housewife mother, has ceased to exist — divorce, working mothers, birth control, and, worst of all, the new birth technology — genetics, transplants, homosexuality and lesbianism. The fear is being increasingly expressed that we are heading for a situation in which the ideal pattern may be one of being married only until the children are grown, with sequential polygamy in the process, and homosexuality (male and/or female) to follow. Group family life may well be the family of tomorrow, the family commune, large groups of people married to each other; with all sorts of variations possible, a family of two husbands and four wives, the institutionalization of wife swapping and group sex.

(c) With urban relocation and industry change, the student of the future may well be more transient than now, frequently changing homes, family and friendship relations.

What emerges from all this is the vast cost of these experiments to limited numbers of pupils. The university without walls linking thirty or so individual colleges around Antioch College in the United States had approximately 2,000 students in 1972 all doing individual work. The weekend college associated with Long Island University began in 1971 with twenty-two courses and 241 students; it now has 2,500 students and offers five degree programmes at the undergraduate and graduate level with more than 160 courses per session; it operates on a tuition reduction plan for spouses and encourages the participation of children through a special programme in a private school in Long Island. Much of this development is centred on the vast cultural resources provided by large towns such as Philadelphia, Chicago or New York.

It is immediately obvious that such costs and such expensive diversions are beyond the scope of developing countries which now find themselves in a quandary in respect of the utter confusion that prevails in the field of education in general and in the field of higher education in particular.

Certain fundamental conclusions emerge from the analysis above of the dichotomy in education between the developed and the developing countries.

1. The World Bank's pessimistic forecast of the prospects for Indepen-

dencia and the developing countries of which it is a hypothetical proto-type is likely to get worse rather than better, for the following principal reasons:

(a) The GNP will not improve. The World Bank itself contrasted (in 1974) the anticipated annual increase of GNP up to 1980 by 8.4 per cent for seven OPEC countries and the annual decrease of GNP by 0.4 per cent for ten developing countries with a per capita GNP of less than $200. The 'dichotomy' is almost certainly much more pronounced in 1977. We have already witnessed the catastrophic decline in sugar prices, certain to be further and more adversely affected by the inroads of HFCS (High Fructose Corn Sweetners) in America and the research in Europe based on wheat starch.

(b) The rate of population growth will further worsen the adverse balance. Not one of the educationally least advanced countries has a rate of natural increase as low as the *highest* rate recorded in the educa-tionally most advanced countries. UNESCO considers the dividing line at a gross reproduction rate of 2 per cent per annum, that is, doubling in less than thirty-five years; most developing countries have growth rates exceeding 2.5 per cent per annum, that is, doubling in twenty-eight years. As one analyst puts it, 'With the continued rapid increase in the school-age population in the developing countries, it will require an increase of 50 per cent in schooling facilities in about fifteen years *just to maintain the enrolment rates at the existing level*'. The United Nations has asserted the basic human right that couples may decide on the number and spacing of their children, and must have adequate education and information to enable them to do so. If this supersedes religious doctrine to the contrary, it most emphatically does not condone compulsory sterilization.

(c) The sheer costs of the education system militate against the narrowing of the gap between developed and developing. A distin-guished Caribbean scholar, Arthur Lewis, stated some ten years ago that 'while the average salary of a primary school teacher is less than 1½ times per capita national income in the United States, a primary school teacher gets three times the per capita national income in Jamaica, five times in Ghana and seven times in Nigeria'. At secondary education level, he added, cost per teacher was thirty times per capita income in Nigeria and twelve times in Jamaica, as compared with twice in the United States. Lewis calculated that to give eight years of primary education to every child would cost in terms of the national income as follows: USA, 0.8 per cent; Jamaica, 1.7 per cent; Ghana, 2.8 per cent; Nigeria, 4 per cent. An unweighted average for all countries with avail-able data shows the following percentages of teachers' salaries to total recurrent costs: Africa, 71 per cent; Asia, 73 per cent; Latin America, 72 per cent. There are other costs to be considered. The new mathe-matics teaching cost US$5 million in two years, with an equal amount on physics teaching. Nigeria has recently abolished the new mathe-matics, describing it as 'a device to enslave us to computers'.

(d) Foreign aid is a delusion. The USSR member of the 1972 UNESCO Commission has stated that the much-touted programme of devoting 1 per cent of the GNP of developed countries in aid to developing countries 'is only justified in the case of developed countries which derived enormous profits during the colonial period from exploiting, and which often still do exploit, the developing countries of today. On the other hand, it should not under any circumstances be required of the socialist countries, whose aid to the Third World cannot be regarded as a kind of indemnity tied to some fixed percentage.'

(e) The brain drain compounds the frustration of the developing countries. With limited resources they train their specialists only to have them emigrate to the developed countries or fail to return home if they had been sent abroad to study. It reminds one of that poetic alliteration describing the labour of Sisyphus — 'up a high hill he heaves a huge round stone'; only to see it come tumbling down when it was near the top. As of 1966, of the 6,773 scientists and engineers who were admitted into the US as immigrants, 1,825 came from Asia excluding Japan, and 843 from America excluding Canada. Admittedly this is a problem also for the developed countries — 1,251 in 1966 came from the United Kingdom, 1,105 from Canada, 673 from the EEC. But 33 per cent of foreign scientists living in the US and 16 per cent of those living in Canada come from developing countries. The cost of all this, even restricting it to money terms, can be gauged from the United Kingdom calculation — it cost (1967) £6,000 to train a BSc in engineering sciences. Emigration represents a loss to the British economy (actual value of his professional career) of £30,000. His value for the American economy which he enters, however, is about £78,000.

2. The experience of the last 500 years of global history constitutes a warning to the developing countries which they should never forget. Two considerations emerge here:

(a) Scientific thought and tradition in the Western world, fortified by the teachings of the Christian religion, in appraising and analysing blackness, black men, other non-white men, were adamant on their inferiority even to the point where their very humanity could be challenged. What Winthrop Jordan, in his classic *White over Black*, calls 'rational science and irrational logic', was so pervasive in the seventeenth and eighteenth centuries of slavery and racism that it contaminated so pre-eminent a naturalist as Linnaeus and normally so sensible a philosopher as Buffon. In both cases the problem was miscegenation. Linnaeus, originally a firm advocate of the fixity of species, came to accept hybridization of plants. When it came to human beings, that was a different matter. Linnaeus thought instinctively of the blacks and saw in it 'the most frightful conclusions'. Buffon lent the weight of his prestige in the most casual manner to the contemporary association of blacks and apes, particularly in the form of black women and male apes. The later Victorian fixation with the notion of a 'missing link' was an essential component of the craniometry so devastatingly used to denigrate and degrade not blacks alone but all non-whites, until racism was forced to retreat when it was demonstrated that Japanese, Amerindians, Eskimos, Polynesians frequently had brains larger than Europeans. With this long tradition going down to the IQ tests of the Americans, developing countries and their populations could be in very deep trouble indeed in respect of genetic engineering as it is progressing in the advanced countries.

(b) On the political side, the whole history of the past 500 years has been the ruthless rejection of non-whites by the races of Europe − from the Spanish Conquest of the New World down to this day. Where democratic ideas took root, two policies emerged (i) as in the United States, the mudsill theory of society, blacks (and others) to do the dirty work; (ii) in Australia, New Zealand, Canada, 'keep the breed pure', in the words of Australia's labour movement. The white worker was in the vanguard of what we today call apartheid, from the time when Spanish artisans sought to keep Amerindians out of their guilds. The hysteria in Australia against everybody − blacks, Hindus, Chinese, Japanese; the campaign in California against Asians; the almost ludicrous efforts to keep Vancouver white and prevent Chinese workers and Hindu farmers; these seem almost incredible today against the hordes of illiterate, backward, penniless immigrants to America and Oceania from various areas of Europe. Today the racial confrontation is very much in evidence, and not alone in South Africa and Rhodesia. The developed (white) countries have all the advantages − nuclear capability, very high GNP, superior educational structures and methods, science and technology to command. Must they have still one more − that, as the political struggle for equality is being intensified, the developed countries should rule out history as irrelevant, suppress 1776 and all that, take in a few token scientists and engineers from the developing countries as the hewers of wood and drawers of water of today, and simply wipe out all ancient indignities and deprivations as obsolete and immaterial? In their higher education developments, whatever they might be, the developing countries will at their peril discard the humanities and consign history to the waste paper basket. They need only recall the computer history of slavery presented recently in *Time on the Cross*.

Against this background what are the alternatives available to developing countries if they are to pursue some form of higher education?

Universities? Many of them have already chosen that route and adopted various models. Many of them will now surely advise against that route or suggest care and caution in the choice of model. Many of them have departed from the guideline that a GNP of $600 million was a minimum base upon which to sustain a university in a developing country with an ideal closer to $1,000 million. In 1966 Sierra Leone with a GNP of $160 million had a university of 800 students; Liberia with $228 million had a 600-student university. Mauritius had fifty-eight students with a GNP of

$159 million. Limited and forced efforts and the experiences of countries like these, ten years after, in sustaining the growth and quality of university type education could be useful to many developing countries.

The Caribbean experience particularly has its lessons. A university established some twenty-five years ago within the pattern of the colonial tradition. A study by learned foreign experts and a set of recommendations made with little reference to needs, resources or aspirations except to denounce them. A model copied from England even to the ridiculous details of having its terms called Michaelmas, Hilary and Trinity; and its degrees conferred by London University on the basis of a curriculum so English that its literature course required Old and Middle English. A model which assumes the need for a long 'summer' vacation in an area where there is summer all the year around and results in millions of dollars of plant and facilities not being utilized for at least three months each year. A model which insists on adoption of the 'residential' concept, although capital resources are only available to support some 15 to 20 per cent of the student population at the Halls of Residence.

A school of medicine now in its twenty-fifth year and having produced over 1,000 doctors mainly for employment outside of the Caribbean. A Faculty of Engineering that over the past twelve years has produced over 700 graduate engineers — not a *single one* in agricultural engineering, not a *single one* in petroleum engineering, not a *single one* in mining engineering. Agriculture, petroleum and bauxite are the mainstays of the economies of the Caribbean. A Faculty of Agriculture that, in spite of its previous reputation for excellence in its colonial context, has had great difficulty attracting its quota of students and to this date has not yet produced 400 graduates.

Indeed, there are lessons to be learnt about the planning of a university and controlling its development. Even the opportunity to demonstrate to the world that a university, of all things, could exist on a regional basis was not fully grasped, and now the full effects of fragmentation are being witnessed — a school of tourism in one island, some form of medical training in another, and who knows what to come elsewhere – a casino school to cater to the casino environment? The combination of the inability of the smaller Caribbean islands to meet increasing costs and the divergence between the contributing territories in respect of the priorities to be pursued have resulted in Trinidad and Tobago, with its stronger economic and financial position due to hydrocarbons, deciding to proceed out of its own funds to finance particular expansions, if even under the umbrella of the university. Examples are: (a) a new medical faculty located in Trinidad financed regionally, but with the addition of dentistry and nursing as priorities from the Trinidad and Tobago point of view and therefore financed locally; (b) a doubling of the intake in the Faculty of Engineering; (c) a doubling of the output in respect of the Faculty of Education. In addition there are extra-university developments directly under Trinidad and Tobago control and financial responsibility in such areas as petroleum, banking and accountancy.

Should developing countries follow the Indian pattern and deliberately, at all costs and sacrifices, establish a limited number of 'centres of excellence' and relate these to the national effort?

Are there other alternatives not yet fully explored or not yet discovered?

Can developing countries afford the luxury of devoting substantial resources to institutions that traditionally become isolated from the rest of the society and cater for a selected few? If their clientele cannot boast of the affluence of student dissent elsewhere, they still represent an elite in the developing countries in relation to the poverty of the primary and secondary levels; can they then be permitted the luxury of dissent, strike, disorder of their developed counterparts, squandering the scarce resources that can be used with tremendous impact elsewhere in the society? On the other hand, can they afford not to establish and sustain some carefully chosen form of higher education?

There are many approaches that need to be more fully explored. Work and study programmes embracing not just the professional areas but all areas and all forms of activity; adult and continuing education; universities that extend to the community rather than consume the resources of the community in the establishment and maintenance of large plant; universities that integrate higher education with secondary education and 'adopt' the secondary schools; universities that recognize the technology of mass communication without eroding the professor—student relationship. University without walls, university of the air, open-admissions policies — the developing countries must look to some of these concepts and experiments if alternatives in higher education are to be carefully chosen.

The pressures on developing countries in other areas more related to survival — health, population control, food, energy, literacy, unemployment — are such that there is the continuing danger that models for higher education are accepted easily and without caution. The lessons of the past warn against this. In the final analysis, whatever alternatives appear, a developing country should ask itself, does it really need any of such alternatives, and then proceed with the greatest caution.

In these days of ideological obsessions in the developing countries, the experience of Bolivia suggests a basic caution, that the 'reformers' are too intellectual. The following dialogue between guerrillas and one of the peasants is instructive:

'When the National Liberation Army triumphs,' they said, 'you will have tractors, schools and even a university.'
'What's a university?' asked the peasant;
    The spokesman for the guerrillas replied that it was a place where high school students went to study.
'And who are high school students?'
'Those who have finished secondary school'.
'And where are they going to come from?'
"They will have to come from you yourselves.'

Chapter 4

Industry and higher education alternatives

P. Holroyd and D. J. Loveridge

'Education will be a fundamental part of modernization only if it is geared to the attitudinal changes required for this purpose, especially the individual and collective responsibilities of the people themselves. . . .'
Albert Lauterbach

'Education fits a person for life,' runs the long-held axiom, but what sort of life? For through this axiom the educational institutions are tacitly allotted a degree of clairvoyance concerning the future, denied to all others save the Church. Academic institutions plead that their programmes are based on what society perceives its needs to be, but how many people participate directly in developing the educational response to the likely future needs of societies?

The past two or three decades have seen a considerable change in the role of education, parallel with the growth of technology and the technologically-based society. An increasing demand has been placed on academic institutions to produce relevant, useful contributions to the wealth and growth prospects for society, and this they have clearly achieved in the developed world. In Japan, for example, an almost universal linking of industrial needs to the output of higher education has been created, while America and Europe have seen a very close correspondence develop between industrial growth, the consumer society and educational norms. At no point during the period has the consequence of a major decline in industrial growth potential been assessed as an issue concerning the developed world's way of life.

Most definitions of education illustrate sharply the differing emphasis between education and learning; contrast the dominance of the formative preparation in early life associated with education, with the non-specific age for the acquisition of knowledge, which is learning. During recent times much stress has been placed on the need for some re-training, to fit people with new skills to replace old and outworn skills. The principle of lifelong learning, which is made explicit in the principle of re-training, seems to be at odds with the definition and the reality of education based on one kind of working life.

Do we need education or the ability to learn 'how and what' to learn? Not in any sense does this imply some form of learning through free expression, but rather that education should imbue the individual with the knowledge of how learning proceeds, so that he/she may be prepared for lifelong learning as individual needs, and those of society, change. Such a theme is likely to be one plank in the base of a stable society, because it is likely to disperse, and later avoid, massive blocs of people whose skills are passing into obsolescence, and who have a resistance to learning 'something new' rooted in their education. What is education really about? A serf society requires little education except that passed from the ruling class to their descendants. An agricultural society requires education principally in farming methods, probably best achieved from direct experience in the field; that is, education by contact. A craft society requires education in developing expertise, probably best achieved by apprenticeships and perhaps some element of craft schools, because the craft school is a more efficient mode of transferring know-how to the greater numbers involved in a craft society. An industrial society requires education to provide a great variety of skills associated with an industrial complex, not only skills of the worker or the craftsman, but also the skills of the supporting functions, which we now call 'services' and 'organizing functions.' For example, *management* requires more mind skill than hand skill. Many such skills in science, engineering, marketing, accounting and so on, have only become necessary during the past fifty years and higher education has been hard pressed, but valiant, in its attempt to supply the growing demand for these diverse talents. Specialized institutions have grown to create managers, engineers, designers, etc., geared to the believed needs of society.

Some of these innovative forces are already at work in embryo. The complex design needs for computer systems, the institutionalization of technology assessment, the growth of the knowledge industry and the emphasis on neighbourhood help, autonomy or self-reliance establishments, are examples of these forces. The main role of education in our changing society must be to awaken and develop the sense of interdependent influences, so that these can be used as forces for good, rather than overwhelming forces for confusion and chaos as they are at present. Interdependence is the central issue we wish to examine as an alternative theme behind higher education, a theme which is consistent with the way society and industry are developing.

Is there then a crisis in education? Falling standards in literacy, numeracy and academic achievement are often cited.[1] The decrease in the proportion of students taking science and technology is often quoted as a concern closely aligned to the apparent unattractiveness of industry as a career and the misuse of graduates by industry. The cry of relevance has been raised and listened to, perhaps to the detriment of quality and gumption,[2] and is now being followed by talk of a deliberate attempt at social manipulation in an endeavour to make science, technology and industry more attractive as routes and destinations through higher education.[3] Bearing in mind the emphasis on learning, are these matters the essence of the crisis in education? Here crisis has the connotation of a turning point, not of imminent collapse. In this sense, the crisis in education stems from a growing expectation of learning to cope with great complexity in the human and the natural world, and the reality of our failure to achieve this. We regard this as due to 'education's' belief in separateness in compartmentality, in specialisms and in the process of analysis. The crisis may be summarized as the clash of interrelated dependence versus specialization in separateness, and typified perhaps by the generalist versus specialist dichotomy. The principles of interrelatedness and lifelong learning, require both the generalist and the specialist to fuse and to develop a continual dialogue, based on mutually understood principles of learning.

Why is so much emphasis now placed on interrelatedness? Surely throughout history, through the family, the formation of settlements, the pillage and plunder of war, and through honest and not-so-honest trading, mankind's activities and their environment have been interrelated? Granted that this is true, the new interrelatedness stems from the magnitude of mankind's activities, and the increased frequency and velocity of the relationships under the stimulus of technology. The old juxtaposition of social need and trade (or economic activity as it later became) has become reversed, with the transformation of social needs to social wants, in an endeavour to placate the remorseless economic engine. It is this scale, frequency and velocity of interrelationships which is new, transforming a world of individual, but lowly connected settlements into a highly connected global village. There are causes for concern here: for example, crop failure in the United States threatens famine in India and higher prices (and inflation) in many other countries increasing the imbalance in worldwide wealth; the political scope for technology-based terrorism; the international political and legal aspects of ocean or sea-floor management; growing decay in cities, growing waste disposal problems, our growing crime rates and so on. All these act together to create a marked impression on the individual, especially among the young whose life style is yet to be established. Communication technology has increased, and continues to increase the interconnectedness and of the various factors making up our global society and has created a dependency upon diverse services; these are now essential to many modes of living in the developed world, which is locked into this system, whether it likes it or not. The web so created makes everyone vulnerable to the crises previously regarded as remote or irrelevant. Interrelatedness across the globe in a time span as short as, or shorter than, that which used to pertain for interaction across the settlement, alters the form of knowledge needed to conduct human affairs. The old principles of regarding each settlement, each country as autonomous have to be modified in the face of the global dependencies which are now evident. Much greater emphasis is needed on geopolitical interrelatedness where the geographical part expresses concern for the relationships between climate, food production, raw materials distribution, population distribution, industrial activity, ecology, etc., while the political part embraces the values, the norms and the social political—economic aspirations of the different parts of the world and of a nation.

The emphasis on learning and interrelatedness is deliberate since neither forms a conscious part of education now. However, three questions arise from this emphasis:

1. How quickly can knowledge be diffused?
2. How quickly does it become irrelevant?

3. How should learning be conducted to enable diffusion and irrelevance to be coped with simultaneously?

Theories of diffusion have been developed, but counterparts for irrelevance seem not to have been considered. The balance indicated by 3 above, cannot therefore exist (all knowledge is thus assumed to be useful for all time) and learning most likely becomes haphazard. Learning about interrelatedness must then be as concerned, if not more concerned with what is irrelevant as with the converse. The conscious perception of irrelevance requires emphasis since it begins to permit the possibility of some decoupling between settlements or nations, in a situation of increasing connectedness. In this way, perception of irrelevance is, perhaps, a second plank to a stable society.

Decoupling has another aspect deeply enmeshed with education. All too often education is thought of as a prerogative of the developed world. Of course this is not so, and the relationships between education as part of a national culture and education as a part of geopolitical interaction, needs to be understood. Geoffrey Vickers has described the concept of a global culture as 'mind boggling' and has gone on to highlight the reality of the 'passionate fission' of larger nation states into a proliferation of smaller ones.[4] Examples abound in Africa, whilst the Basque separatist movement, devolution proposals in the UK, and the Quebec separatist movement in Canada, indicate how widespread are the growing pressures for the creation of smaller cultural entities and for some decoupling between them.

The major shift in the societal trends towards greater autonomy is most marked in the development of youthful organizations, communes, university societies, protection societies for freedom, and particularly of community pressure and action groups, whose concern is towards reducing over-control.

Joseph Needham has said 'Western philosophy tended to regard reality as substance whereas Eastern philosophy tended to regard reality as relation'.[5] The distinction between 'reality as substance' and 'reality as relation', which Needham sees as a Western versus Eastern view, can also be regarded as a developing distinction between the past and future views of education. Our society is generally regarded as more complex, more interdependent and more sensitive to disturbance than formerly. Understanding relationships is clearly becoming more important and urgent, yet this understanding is not urged or pursued effectively; without it we cannot move towards creating a true knowledge industry. The history of civilization is, in part, the story of increasingly complex artifacts. The manipulation of materials according to acquired knowledge has led man from the stone age to the electronics age. The well-being and wealth of people in the developed countries, seems to be directly linked to the 'knowledge content' of our products and processes. Within our developed societies this relationship has been recognized by the creation of 'technical knowledge transfer organizations'; these are schools, colleges, universities, institutes and the like, whose purpose is to provide an adequate supply of high-grade knowledge by simply short circuiting the induction period that is normally undergone in a learning sequence. Preformed knowledge can be pumped into people, effectively eliminating the time-consuming aspect of the synthesis of data and information. However arts, crafts and the traditional industrial activities, still require the 'synthesis' approach of a long-term apprenticeship. In other fields the rate of acquisition of new data, information and the creation of knowledge, is such that a university training in a speciality no longer equips a person for a lifetime's work, and so renders the 'knowledge transfer' institutions inadequate. Industry faces an opportunity, a necessity even, to prepare for considerable retraining programmes for its own viability and also to maintain the cultural fabric and, by doing this, to obtain some return on any capital expended in generating transferable knowledge. Any company which can do this must be considered to be part of knowledge industry.

Given that some structural change is inevitable in industry, what part should industry play in creating the new forms of learning institution, (which may include the knowledge industries) that may be needed? Are the educational institutions already creating these new forms themselves? The answer to the second question is a qualified 'yes', particularly in the USA where there are several hundred learning programs with a futures basis. In the UK the situation is quite different, with only two or three such courses being attempted. The situation in other countries is even less clear, although a futures directory now being compiled may help to clarify the situation. A similar pattern exists in the formation of futures orientated learning companies. In the UK the first such companies are being formed or are under discussion;[6] these activities should not be confused with conventional consultancies, which of necessity operate in the mould of the current paradigms of industrial society.

Where then does education, particularly higher education, fit in to this complex picture of the future? There is, unfortunately, a strongly developed trend for the diffusion of knowledge (which subsequently becomes a basis for education) to occur without applying tests of cultural relevance. More often the knowledge is introduced in spite of its cultural incompatibility. The current 'passionate fission' indicates the need for a greater appreciation of the role of geopolitics in establishing patterns that result in a matching of new knowledge and traditional cultures. Such an appreciation would allow developing nations to evolve new cultural forms at a far greater rate than can be achieved in the developed countries, where the amount of unlearning needed is far higher. It is not the prerogative of new knowledge to attempt to bring about cultural uniformity in line with the values and norms of the nations supplying the knowledge. One of the alternatives for higher education is to promote an error-accepting mode of enquiry[7] necessary for the building of new forms of culture, and to de-emphasize the destruction of cultures through the enforced adoption of inappropriate knowledge. In this sense the educators (or purveyors of knowledge) will need to convey the art of learning, rather than to give instruction (a form of conditioning), if a strong motivation towards self-help is to be developed into a norm within a society. Cultural variety, which is associated with education and learning, is evidently growing whilst cultural convergence, is not.

The change occurring in society towards 'relation', towards more meaningful aspects of existence, towards the 'essence' of things, has partly come about because of the saturation of the developed Western world with goods and materials. It is natural, therefore, that there should be a revival of interest in the aspects of living which are considerably less material, and more spiritual than we have seen for some time. Schumacher[8] urges Buddhist economics, whilst other aspects of intermediate technology seem to be becoming more relevant to the developed world, as the purely materialistic economic climate is seen to be less relevant, while Illich[9] vigorously challenges many of the contemporary views of our society. Higher education will need to come to terms with this shift in interests, because its role in the past has been to serve the technical/materialistic needs of cultures. It is now clear that society's needs in the developed world can only decreasingly sustain continued growth from the present level. A change from a society of processing and producing, towards a society which can consider the relationships, the well-being, the 'eudemony' as Stafford Beer refers to it,[10] of people, seems to have started. Perhaps this may be more important economically in the longer term, than the behaviour of our current society.

The foregoing implies that higher education will need to shift its emphasis, from that of providing relevant academic disciplines supporting *current* activities, towards universal, holistic aspects aiding the needs of people, particularly towards self-help and autonomy. In other words higher education will need to broaden its base, to encompass the desires of those people who are perceiving the reality of change and who wish to comprehend the very complex concerns of a changing society. Higher education needs to change its goal from 'immediate relevance', that is, providing more electronic engineers, geologists, sociologists and so on, but rather see its goal as creating people who can derive solutions in societies to issues which are highly interrelated across the society and its environment.

Education, and particularly higher education has to retain credibility. It has long been portrayed as a rational logical process typical of the age, but is it? The realization that the education process and science are not value free is now widespread, and may be exemplified by the many changes and discoveries brought about by no more than a belief that events are not as they are explained by current paradigms; this is the Kuhnian paradigm shift.[11] It is necessary for learning to come to grips with the concepts of uncertainty and alternatives if it is to become future related; these are two of the most important attributes of the error-accepting mode of enquiry, which allows learning to remain credible even though it is not value free.

For industry, the theme of learning and error-acceptance implies that education needs to become more future orientated. Equally awkward is the development of thinking in breadth, in terms of interrelationships over a consciously wide framework, without sacrificing the quality and gumption that goes with, and is essential to the mastery of a specialism. It must be twenty years (at least) since it was declared that the age of the competent generalist had arrived and that education should reflect that need. In fact the age of the competent generalist hardly seems to have arrived today, and the pathway to generalism must still be largely through self-learning. Structural change in industry is also much discussed and, presuming the phrase to mean 'new work in new industries' rather than 'old work in a restyled industry', introduces the educational need referred to earlier namely, learning how to learn, and learning which is related to the role of graduates in the presently unknown industries of the future. The new roles are hard to discern with any degree of certainty, but it seems reasonably certain that many of them are likely to lie in those areas of human activity concerned with the fundamentals of life: survival, security, belongingness on the Maslovian hierarchical scale.[12] Indeed the educational task of creating a world of self-actualizers is as mind boggling as Geoffrey Vickers's concept of a uniform culture mentioned earlier. Just as one requires the elimination of cultural variety the other (universal self-actualization) requires the creation of enormous new cultural variety in a way which might prove incompatible with an industrial society. Both would require very great cultural change. As well as serving a society's basic needs for agriculture, for crafts, for production and for services, we shall surely see a growing need for education to make 'visible the invisible technologies', as Buckminster Fuller calls them,[13] or to demystify society, as Ivan Illich[14] puts it. In both instances the principle is to make clear to the individual how artifacts and society work, rather than have these important phenomena shrouded in the 'black box' syndrome.

Within the education system itself there is a considerable degree of compartmentalization, which will need to be broken down if we are to be effective in resolving the problems in the future. The barriers to this order of change seem almost insurmountable. The institution of higher education has evolved into a self-sustaining system; it cannot be regarded as an adaptive system. Although exotic experiments have been made in the last decade or two at an elementary level this does not imply that the form of education has become future related. In some ways the willingness to undertake major shifts in elementary education on the basis of political dogma can only cause dismay, even though education is recognized as not being 'value free'. It is essential that higher education assists the formation of a philosophic framework within which society can operate; there is a sense in which all institutions must rest upon that which is believed, and seen, to be fundamental, real and true. When institutions depart from this fundamental position then there is a move away from the true meaning of legitimacy. As societies develop and change there will be shifts in values and norms. Nevertheless, education, and particularly higher education, must stand upon a bedrock of fundamentals that allows the learning being pursued to be of value to the society no matter how it evolves. No society will remain static in a world where interconnectedness is already high and will become yet higher. The resulting dichotomy of a search for individual autonomy in an interdependent world leads to the need for learning how to balance the new collective responsibilities and restraints, and, the need for personal freedom. To the extent that precise solutions to concerns of this kind can no longer be entertained, we require people educated in a way of thinking which can operate not only at a specific, relevant level, but at levels which stretch beyond the immediate moment and situation; this, higher education is not achieving nor attempting to pursue.

What then is likely to be the content of a learning course at a higher education level? Michael McDaniel[15] illustrated one possible response to this question by suggesting a course which would help *maturing* individuals:

>   to cope with their society
>   to understand themselves
>   to understand their investment in the future
>   not to feel powerless or impotent
>   to identify with the society they will inherit
>   to understand the nature of change
>   to see the means of affecting the direction of change
>   to understand key social science concepts and their relation to change
>   to identify roles they can take in the change process
>   to avoid ethno-centralism
>   to incorporate classroom learning into their immediate environments
>   to transform classroom learning to future responsibilities

and would help *mature* individuals:

>   to assist maturing individuals to create relevant learning situations
>   to understand the role of maturing individuals in change
>   to connect with and become involved with maturing individuals

and would help *mature* and *maturing* individuals change immature institutions.

Our own approach to learning is based on six themes: social, technical, ecological, economic, political and values. The mode of learning is thematic and involves both ways of considering irrelevance and Popper's philosophy of criticism[16] to ensure a growth in knowledge. The themes of learning are constantly related to one another to provide a way of understanding interrelatedness in an effort to identify possible forces for change and their outcomes. These, being future related, constitute the initial step in synthesizing alternatives for the future. Many aids are employed in this mode of learning, including trend projection and historical views. The mode is fundamentally error-accepting and it understands that the full set of alternatives for the future can never be specified. We see little evidence of such forms of learning developing in the formal educations system· indeed they may never do so.

Future excellence begins in the formative years, particularly during the period of higher education, when growing maturity enables a growing appreciation of the philosophical basis of culture. It is culture which defines how society works, through the explicit and tacit axioms of behaviour (values and norms as defined by Geoffrey Vickers[17]), these uncompromisingly absorb the content of the learning themes quoted earlier, thus refuting those who would have us believe that excellence can only be attained through specialism. Philosophy (and hence culture) is never stationary, it is continuously driving the engine of change. Future excellence then depends upon the encouragement of future-orientated learning.

Industries and nations have but two sources of real wealth: the skill of their people and the raw materials within their geographical confines. For many nations the latter source of wealth is diminishing; skill, which represents learning associated with error-acceptance, is then the remaining plank of a dynamic, future-orientated culture. To ignore the continual development of future orientated skills is to sow the seeds of cultural and economic decline.

The authors wish to thank the Directors of Pilkington Brothers Limited and Dr D. S. Oliver, Director of Research and Development, for permission to publish this paper. The views expressed are those of the authors alone and are not those of the Company.

References

1. C. B. Cox, and R. Boysen, *The Fight for Education: Black Paper 1975* Dent, 1975.
2. R. Pirsig, *Zen and the Art of Motorcycle Maintenance*, Bodley Head, 1974.
3. J. Callaghan, *Financial Times* Report, December 1976.
4. Geoffrey Vickers, From a speech to the first Ashridge Conference on 'How do we use futures thinking', 6 November 1976.
5. J. Needham, *Science and Civilization in China*, Cambridge University Press, 1956.
6. Anon, SRC Report on Teaching Companies, 1976.
7. Donald Michael, *On Learning to Plan and Planning to Learn*, Jossey-Bass, San Francisco, 1973.
8. E. F. Schumacher, *Small is Beautiful*, Abacus, Sphere Books, 1974.
9. Ivan Illich, *Tools for Conviviality*, Fontana, 1975.
10. Stafford Beer, *Platform for Change*, Wiley, 1975.
11. Thomas Kuhn, 'The structure of scientific revolutions', *International Encyclopedia of Unified Science*, Vol, 2, No. 2, 1962.
12. A. Maslow, *Motivation and Personality*, Harper & Row, New York, 1954.
13. Buckminster Fuller, 'An operating manual for spaceship earth', *Environment and Change*, 1973.
14. Ivan Illich, 'De-schooling Society', Harper & Row, New York. 1971.
15. Michael McDaniel, 'Tomorrow curriculum today' from *Learning for Tomorrow: The Role of the Future in Education*, A. Toffler (ed.), Vintage Books, Random House, New York, 1974.
16. Karl Popper, *Objective Knowledge*, Oxford University Press, London, 1972.
17. Geoffrey Vickers, *Making Institutions Work*, Assoc. Bus. Prog. Ltd, 1973.

Chapter 5

The mass media and higher education

Brian Groombridge

Despite the success of the Open University, the juxtaposition of the two phrases 'higher education' and 'the mass media' is still somewhat dissonant to British ears. There is felt to be an incompatibility between the quality implied by 'higher' and the quantity suggested by 'mass'. There is more to this suspicion than snobbery, though part of it is snobbish. It also comes from an awareness of a profound culture gap between the demanding world of academic rigour (attentive to detail, slow to generalize, sensitive to the protocol governing relations between one discipline and another), and the indulgent world of the mass media (trading in stereotypes, quick to oversimplify, promiscuously flouting subject divisions). And whatever their many failings in practice, educational institutions must always strive for the development of the individual student, seeking the keys which liberate particular individuals, seeking both the best substance for them and the optimum pace at which growth is possible. The mass media, by definition, address themselves to masses. Programmes, scheduled and timed to the second, reach millions simultaneously; editions run into thousands. These media are like supermarkets, and have much the same virtues and disadvantages.

Indeed, the very success of the Open University may have contributed to the reinforcement of this feeling of antithesis, rather than of partnership, between the two domains. Everyone knows that the Open University was first mooted as a 'University of the Air', a parvenu enterprise with ambitions, as the popular press had it at the time, to equip housewives with degrees as they did the dusting.[1,2] Now the Open University has arrived. It is a proper university. Its work is manifestly of the highest quality. Its officers wear medieval robes; it has a charter, even a mace, and it has, accordingly, put television in its place. Its students, who have actually to be more literate than most, only spend 5 per cent of their time watching programmes.[3,4]

Some appreciation of this antithesis, at least of a tension if not a melodramatic conflict between the proclaimed values of higher education and the demonstrated values of the mass media, is useful. It is a protection against projects which seem to look towards a world in which educational equality might be achieved by producing multiple copies of diplomas on the required scale. But such an awareness is not in itself a fruitful guide to policy, and never was. We now have in any case to take stock of a good deal of cohabitation.

International experience

The Americans were, understandably, the pioneers. Chicago's trail-blazing Television College was, in a sense, a venture which related some of the skills of nearby Detroit to the work of higher education. Other countries, with huge distances to cover, were, also understandably, among the first to follow suit. In 1961, the University of New South Wales opened the first Australian radio station to be used exclusively for education. In 1966, a television station was added. Both have been responsible ever since for professional updating courses. Despite a strong feeling in the faculty of the Memorial University of Newfoundland in favour of personal contact between tutors and students, the university has had and used broadcast-standard equipment since 1967. Experience in Japan of using correspondence courses in association with broadcasting is leading to the foundation of a major university with broadcasting as its central means of teaching, and its own channel. The Poles have used television to teach advanced mathematics and agricultural studies. Many countries have used broadcasting for the inservice training of teachers and for post-experience courses for other socially important vocations. Early in 1977, the Flemish-speaking Open School, based on Belgian Television, even offered a course for lawyers in cooperation with the professional associations and the Ministry of Justice. The University of California's (San Diego) 'courses by newspaper', syndicated across the United States, are a reminder that 'mass media' include the press; and the exploitation, by universities in the USA and Canada, of programmes originally made in Britain to entertain and interest the general audience, for credit-bearing educational work, indicates that 'broadcasting' in this context does not mean just 'educational broadcasting'. These projects are just a selection from many, all over the world.[5,6,7] They have obviously varied in quality; and sometimes they have reached such small numbers of students that the use of mass media seems hard to justify. But this body of international experience has revealed some fatal incongruity between the ends of higher education and the mass media as means.

The French gave the world the not quite translatable phrase, *éducation permanente*; they have also given us the word '*télé-enseignement*' to describe one way in which *éducation permanente* might be achieved in practice. The Universities of Dijon, Nancy II, Strasbourg II, Besançon and Reims, Metz and Mulhouse (jointly through *l'Entente Universitaire de l'Est*) and several other universities run *Centres de Télé-enseignement Universitaire* (CTUs).

As the new word also suggests, these 'distance learning centres' commonly use television as a way of putting opportunities for university level study before people already in paid employment, or otherwise unable to attend as full-time students. The pedagogical experience of the CTUs, and the history of relations with the French broadcasting authorities, shows that there are real problems to be faced in reconciling higher education and the mass media.[8]

Reaching the mature

The synthetic and synthesizing word '*télé-enseignment*' expresses a unity within which there is struggle. It is also a pointer to what is now seen to be the nub of the issue. In many countries, higher education was a privilege for an elite of young people. Then this tradition was felt to be inequitable and socially short-sighted. More young people could benefit from higher education and society would be the better for it. For the best of democratic motives the nations began to provide academic opportunities for large numbers of men and women too young to benefit from them. These age-cohort batches were then unleashed into economies which found them increasingly difficult to assimilate. The result was as though we had successfully planned for personal frustration, widespread malaise, demonstration and riot, as a dramatic prelude to growing graduate unemployment.

So, many of those available for higher education were not able to benefit from it. Meanwhile, those who were mature enough to benefit from higher education were not available. They were about their adult business — earning a living, looking after children, maintaining houses, running the whole social apparatus. The mass media are relevant to many of the strategies now being devised to bring the constituency (able men and women of all ages) into relation with the resources (institutions of higher education). Learning, as often as not, perhaps more often not, has to be distance learning as well as campus learning, as the boundaries between higher-further-adult-continuing education become blurred, along with distinctions between full-time and part-time students, and between extra- and intra-mural situations.

Mass media are needed, by higher education, as instruments and as partners, because of their capacity to reach geographically dispersed, often otherwise occupied students, and because of their intrinsic power to reach very large numbers of students, and potential students, and the public which is the ultimate patron. It also happens that they have pedagogical virtues of their own. Not least of these is that they operate in public. This stimulates academics and teachers to think more carefully about what they are doing and encourages them to do it well. It also seems possible that because of their popularity, their ubiquitousness and their close connections with the rest of life, their own ambience and contents may sometimes be turned to the advantage of higher education.

Broadcasting and active students

The Open University was designed precisely to make educational resources available to people grown up enough to know what to do with them. This University may have put broadcasting, especially television, in its place, but the place is an important one. The Charter is like most post-war charters in Britain, but is unusual in that it says that the University's objects include 'the advancement and dissemination of learning through teaching and research by a diversity of means such as broadcasting and technological devices appropriate to higher education, by correspondence tuition, residential courses and seminars, and in other relevant ways. . . .'[9]

John Scupham, himself a former Controller of Educational Broadcasting at the BBC, sums up the main functions of broadcasting in these terms:

The nature of those functions has been established in many different contexts. The strength of the broadcast components of Open University courses lies not in their novelty, but in the thoroughness with which they have been integrated with the whole pattern of the teaching. They can be used to make the initial presentation of a series of topics with the maximum impact, leaving the task of development and consolidation to the correspondence teaching, operating through the package. They can highlight or illustrate points of special difficulty. They can be used from time to time to clear up difficulties common to a number of students in the light of student feedback. They can bring the students into contact with first-rate minds, offer them basic documentary material in the social sciences or convey aesthetic experience in ways that lie outside the scope of the more utilitarian package. They can help the university to explain its working and functions, and help students to feel that they are members of a corporate body, and in touch with its teaching staff.[10]

In its second submission to the (Annan) Committee of Enquiry into the Future of Broadcasting, the University listed twenty-four teaching functions for television and another nine for radio. Many of these functions are characteristic of most educational broadcasting — television is used, for example, to demonstrate experiments which depend on large, expensive or inaccessible equipment; to show naturally-occurring events on film; to record interviews with eminent people, and so on. Some functions may be more particular to the Open University — to feed back to students mass results of activities undertaken by students themselves, for example, in less time or more vividly than would be possible in follow-up printed material; or to test students' ability to apply concepts learned from other components of the course. Given the unremitting demands of Open University work and the normality of lethargy as part of the student psyche, one function is of particular importance: to *pace* students; to keep them working regularly; to break inertia of beginning to study in evening.

It is typical of the Open University that it is capable of producing such an analysis of the pedagogical roles of broadcasting.[11] Systematic scrutiny of its own processes is part of the system. This particular analysis is used, operationally, when resources are being allocated and courses planned. It was not prepared for a committee of enquiry. The main burden of the Open University's evidence to Annan was to establish that the present share of BBC channel time was already insufficient for its current needs, and that additional channel capacity (radio and television) would be needed to cope with the University's national expansion and, still more, with its ambition to promote a continuing education programme alongside its existing undergraduate programme.

The role of broadcasting is relatively limited largely because of a shortage of airtime, not just or mainly because of its acknowledged limitations as a teaching medium. Most educational broadcasters believe, with Scupham, that 'Direct teaching by radio or television can undoubtedly be achieved in some subjects for reasonably mature students'.[12] But the received and much reiterated wisdom on all sides is that broadcasting works best when it is part of a complex of related means. The conclusion is not surprising. It is equally true of teachers, or books, or any other medium. They do not work best in isolation.

The more sceptical emphasis about broadcasting as an educator was put in 1963 by Harold Wiltshire, then Professor of Adult Education at the University of Nottingham, in an historically important article in *The Times Educational Supplement*.[13]

Wiltshire had been provoked by the second White Paper on Broadcasting, one consequence of the Pilkington Committee, which, he was convinced, was mistaken in thinking that the difference between 'educative' and 'educational' programmes lay in the latter's being planned systematically and with the benefit of appropriate academic advice. He maintained that programmes could not be educational in themselves. Education depended on taking pains at the reception end to match those at the production end: '. . . a series of television programmes however planned is, like a book or a tape or a film, only the raw material of education. It can, like a book or a tape or a film, be built into an educational process. But as we all know education is a two-way process: it cannot begin, cannot exist, without feedback, without contact between students and tutor. . . .'

He stressed the fundamental difference between 'passive viewers' and 'active *students*' (his emphasis):

Our concern is with students — *those who are prepared to see a series of programmes through and to do whatever accompanying reading, exercises, etc., can be devised. My guess is that the number of such students will be of the order of tens of thousands, not hundreds of thousands. How are we to make contact with them, to put them into touch with some persons who will stand to them in the relation of tutor to students, to get some feedback working?*

His answer to that question was a prospectus which was also a prophesy:

Obviously not by the face-to-face teaching to which most of us are accustomed; our teaching media must become correspondence, special radio programmes supplementing the television programmes, the local press — and one hopes the local or regional meeting. The meagre forces of adult education would need strengthening to tackle such a task, but they would need help of the kind that is fairly easy to provide — administrative, organizing and clerical rather than academic help — for local or regional offices would have to be set up capable of handling the considerable amount of correspondence with students, reproduction of teaching material, marking, certification consultation between adult education organizations, etc., that would obviously be required. But it is not impossible. Could the BBC and the programme companies build something of this kind on to their existing regional organizations? Would not an experiment of this kind attract interest and support from one of our educational trusts?

The upshot was summed up by Phoebe Hall,[14]

A grant was provided by the Leverhulme Trust whereby ATV agreed to produce thirteen twenty-minute programmes on economics. These were transmitted between 27 September and 21 December 1964. Those who enrolled paid a fee, in return for which they were given a handbook and assigned a tutor. The conclusions of the research were published jointly by the National Institute of Adult Education (NIAE) and the University of Nottingham. It was found that a television course could recruit and hold many good students who would not be attracted otherwise. Also, it was found possible to teach effectively through television provided it was coupled with active learning and brought students into contact with tutors. The cost need be no greater than class teaching and, on a larger scale, it could be less. It was not necessary to show programmes on adult education at peak times. Wiltshire and Bayliss argued that 'tele-teaching' should be recognized as a normal method of adult and further education and that a regular service of 'telecourses' should be established under the control of a body of educators: for instance, a National Centre for Broadcasting Education could be formed.

This successful enterprise undoubtedly played a major part in preparing the way for the Open University in practice. Ulster Television and Anglia Television had collaborated respectively with Queen's University, Belfast, and Cambridge University in using television to transmit university lectures (the model which is standard with the French CTUs). These ventures were worth while, and the second, in particular, helped Michael Young, one of the first advocates of a university of the air, to formulate his own vision in practical terms. But the ATV—Nottingham example came much closer to the model adopted by the Open University — a team from the different institutions in partnership jointly prepared a course and its embodying materials (including an unusually sophisticated correspondence course), and a university recruited economics tutors from many and various educational institutions.[15]

I suggested in the 'festschrift' for Emeritus Professor Harold Wiltshire that this innovatory project is of more than historical interest.[16] It has topical significance nearly fifteen years later, especially since the publication of the Venables Report.[17] This report was the final one from a Committee on Continuing Education, set up by the Open University to consider whether and how the University should pursue its other charter responsibility: 'to promote the educational well-being of the community generally'. Venables envisages a pattern of partnerships of many agencies, national, regional and local, and with the Open University itself entering into a wide variety of bilateral and multi-lateral arrangements. Through such coordination, together with appropriate production centres, it is expected that the present fragmentary aggregation of adult education enterprises would begin to make a coherent and versatile system of continuing education.

The report alludes to a range of media and technologies, but once again all references to the mass media are usually in terms of radio and television. These are felt to be of sufficient strategic importance to have a section devoted to them. A key paragraph runs as follows:

On the strength of the existing Open University partnership with the BBC, the Committee sees the value to continuing education of the development of schemes involving broadcasting over and above those which already exist. Regional schemes suggested by ITV interests and the possibility of local radio participation merit investigation as part of regional and local collaborative projects, and the Committee recommends that the University should investigate the desirability and feasibility of establishing regional and local pilot developments involving the appropriate broadcasting agencies. There is some evidence that some sections of the population which the Open University has hitherto had difficulty in reaching through its BBC links could be more readily approached via the Independent Broadcasting networks. It should be remembered that stimulation of interest by means of broadcasting — network, regional or local — may initially, in some circumstances, be more important in introducing people to continuing education than trying to teach them by the same medium.[18]

It is in such a context that experience of the Standard of Living, the so-called 'Nottingham experiment' as it was named at the time, becomes relevant again. That experiment was conducted only in the Midlands, being restricted to the ATV transmission area and never, as it happens, taken by the ITV network. Furthermore, the initiative and master-minding of the project lay with a university. The broadcasting organization was not a mere audiovisual agent (the producer was as much a member of this pre-historic course team as the academics), but neither did it provide the auspices for coordinating and managing the system. The project showed there was an appetite for serious study, at a higher education level, but less demanding in content and duration than first degree work. Wiltshire anticipated much of the Venables Report when he commented at the time in his main report on the project: 'The natural field for television-based teaching may be at a lower than university level, in provision of courses in basic subjects which can serve the needs both of general adult education and at the same time those of students in further education and industrial training.'[19] Such indeed is the basic premise underlying the Open College being debated in the Netherlands and the Open School already in partial operation in Belgium.

'Organizational frameworks'

There are a number of constitutional points of some significance arising from a reconsideration of the Nottingham experiment. The environment is

more propitious for such Open College work now than it was then, simply
because of the Open University's presence. The report is most anxious to
allay suspicions that the University should be harbouring imperialistic
ambitions. The language of partnership and collaboration properly peppers
every page. On the other hand, the universality of the Open University, its
being everywhere and nowhere, enables it to help Britain remedy some of
the many failings caused by having what it was until now correct but com-
placent to describe as 'a national system of education locally administered'. The pattern prescribed by Venables, because it envisages
complementary levels of organization in many permutations, expresses
neither a centralizing Bonapartism nor parochial anarchy and inadequacy.
It is desirable to build in many ways upon the Open University's experience and structure, without thereby concentrating too much power in
Milton Keynes. The Nottingham experiment is a reminder that other
universities could sustain and manage multi-media systems on a regional
basis.

On the other hand, by all accounts the Nottingham experiment would
not have been undertaken and would not have succeeded without the personal enthusiasm of Associated Television's Deputy Chairman, Norman
Collins. Such personal commitment is entirely appropriate in an experiment, but it is no base for substantial and normal provision. The
Nottingham experiment prepared the way for the Open University, but the
main further and adult education effort of the BBC and the independent
television companies did not follow the ATV—Nottingham example (although in recent years much of the BBC's best work has resembled it).
That effort naturally followed the lead of the second post-Pilkington
White Paper, because through that the broadcasters found the clearest and
most authoritative articulation of society's and the government's expectations. The commitment to adult education as defined was expressly
renewed when in 1972 Christopher Chataway, then Minister of Posts,
allowed the broadcasters to decide the hours of broadcasting for themselves. Similarly, although it is known that some members of staff of some
ITV companies, and a substantial body of opinion within the BBC, favour
the development of Open College-like activities with broadcasting as a
chief component, this interest is not a reliable enough foundation for
policy and action. If such developments are to be more than sporadic, they
cannot be expected to depend on the mood of Boards of Governors or on
the even more volatile attitudes of commercial managing directors.
Another round of discussion and agreement with Government is needed
and should follow the Annan Report which was published in March
1977.

It would be politically and educationally harmful for a higher/continuing
education spectrum to be too dependent on the Open University. But it
would also be unwise for it to be too centred on broadcasting, even though
broadcasting organizations have shown that they have the capacity to
mobilize national resources in new patterns of coordination. This risk is
one which is being run in several parts of Europe. However dedicated they

may be to education, broadcasting organizations have other ends. They may sometimes be more responsive to the ideological susceptibilities of government than institutions of higher education should be. Broadcasters like to be doing new things all the time, but the curricula of educational establishments need to be more stable. They also need to be comprehensive, but scarcity of airtime means that even very small colleges can offer a much wider range of courses than the largest broadcasting organizations. Some of these risks, limitations or sheer differences could hamper progress in Scandinavia, Germany and the Low Countries. There ought certainly to be more to an Open College than setting up a high-powered advisory committee, albeit called an 'institute of continuing education', chiefly to enable broadcasters, in tandem with publishers and others, to discharge their statutory educational responsibilities more effectively. The model being contemplated in Finland has much to commend it for those countries which do not wish to invest in new, major institutions like the Open University. The Finns seem likely to urge their universities, in association with the main adult education agencies, to attempt collectively to achieve 'openness' in all the senses intended by the Open University. Broadcasting is seen as a chief means of bringing that openness about.[20]

These issues were anticipated some years ago by some of the most advanced sections of the Russell Report ('Adult Education: A Plan for Development').[21] The Committee wanted a dynamic Development Council for Adult Education for England and Wales. This Council, probably working with the Council for Educational Technology and the National Institute of Adult Education, would foster partnerships between the media and adult education organizations. The Committee foresaw clearly and correctly that the success of the Open University would gradually 'bring into a prominence the need for similar forms of provision at other levels and in non-academic fields'. It also saw that these forms would not be promoted by a range of new organizations. The section is prescient enough to be worth quoting still:

What is desirable is not a super-organisation but an organisational framework. Within such a framework learning systems could be established involving different media and agencies, despite the logistical and organisational problems known to be associated with this kind of enterprise, despite the difficulties that can arise from matters of contract and copyright and from attempts to combine publicly funded institutions with commercial organisations. Even more than this would be possible and necessary; diagnosis of need could be made; curriculum studies carried out, of a kind at present undertaken for adult education only by the Open University at degree course level; and separate institutions brought together for the equivalents of the Open University's course team work.[22]

Open Colleges in Britain (the phrase is more euphonious but more limited in its applications than the ponderous shorthand of the Russell Report — 'modest analogues of the Open University') are more likely to be 'organizational frameworks' than self-standing establishments. Being concerned with all media, according to their pedagogical potential and their convenience to home- and work-based students, would make a venture like 'courses by newspaper' as interesting and valuable in principle as anything with television as lead medium.

Unconventional approaches

The first course by newspaper was called 'America and the Future of Man'. It was developed by Caleb A. Lewis, Director of Special Programs at the University of California (San Diego), who, in 'seeking new ways to make learning attractive to millions of adults who cannot attend school . . . hit upon the idea of bringing college to the students via the newspaper'. 'Lectures' were prepared by eminent academics (including Carl Rogers, the authority on encounter groups, and Dr E. J. Mishan, Professor of Economics at the London School of Economics) and distributed as articles by the 200 newspapers which agreed to take part across the United States. Interested readers could purchase supplementary learning materials (a study guide, annotated bibliography, sources for action, names of relevant congressional committees, a disc containing an orientation talk, a substantial reader and a collection of self tests).

Two hundred universities and colleges accepted the course as valid preparation for credit. 'America and the Future of Man' was followed by two more courses, forming a trilogy culminating in America's bicentennial year.

The enterprising San Diego Extension Division of the University of California has also been active in devising open-learning systems which incorporate or are directly based on broadcasting programmes intended for general consumption. In Britain, its country of origin, the late Jacob Bronowski's 'Ascent of Man' was an outstanding television series. It maintained a tradition of lavishly mounted feature programmes with ambitions, often realized, of providing an intellectual synthesis beyond that of specialist scholars as well as a vivid display in colour and movement beyond the scope of books (although such series are usually accompanied by a handsome book based on the same material). In the United States, its country of adoption, 'Ascent of Man' became a credit course in 300 colleges and universities throughout the country, using the programmes and the book, but, also and crucially, using supplementary print materials. Bearing Harold Wiltshire's distinction in mind, these materials helped convert 'educative' into 'educational' and the metamorphosis of viewers into active students.[23]

The Venables Committee also drew attention to this enterprise:

Much broadcast material is already available in general programmes which may have very considerable educational potential, particularly if it can be developed with back-up material and be used either in recorded form, or distributed well after the original date of transmission. For example, the

Committee was impressed by the development, mainly overseas, of learn-
ing resources based on such projects as the BBC television series Ascent of
Man. It is in fact possible to write a number of courses at any desired levels
of intellectual achievement, based on the same series of broadcasts. Thus,
for example, Open University course broadcasts could be used in
community colleges with wholly different written materials.[24]

The Ontario Educational Communications Authority has made relatively extensive use of programmes made to interest, even to divert, a
general public. It has attempted to precipitate the educational substance
for a range of students by preparing complementary print materials at
widely different levels of academic sophistication. OECA has used not
only high quality feature series with an evidently valuable 'non-fiction'
content by an authority of some renown (it helped finance the BBC series
'The Age of Uncertainty' in which John Kenneth Galbraith's text was
notoriously counterpointed — confused? — by camp visuals as well as more
conventionally illustrated); it has also used serial drama. In 1972 Yorkshire
Television presented an elegant and witty series by Philip Mackie about
office life called 'The Organisation'. OECA has used it as a resource to
illustrate the sociology of industry, bureaucracy, hierarchy and similar
topics. It has even commissioned Dr James Dator, the futurologist and
author of 'Eutopia', to write the text to accompany episodes from the
family viewing fantasy serial 'Dr Who'.

Some of these examples may evoke the worst fears of many a guardian
of the academic mysteries. It is undoubtedly true, as Sir Walter Perry
warns elsewhere in this volume, that 'attempts to base a written course on
a pre-existing broadcasting component, designed originally for a different
purpose, can succeed but are often very unsatisfactory'. It is also true that
whereas the Open University can usually point to objective measures by
which to indicate 'success' or 'unsatisfactoriness', much of this innovatory
activity has not always been accompanied by matching research and
evaluation. The Russell Report was wise to recommend that the Development Council for Adult Education should 'arrange for the monitoring of
the operation of the multi-media courses in order to build up a body of
experience of their working'.[25] It would be in the spirit of the Venables
Report for the Institute of Educational Technology of the Open
University to form alliances with other higher education establishments
and the Council for Educational Technology. Such a partnership could
provide a research service in parallel with the multi-media, inter-agency
course provision services which it also recommends.

The beginnings of a substantial agenda for such a research body are
already apparent. More needs to be known at the level of systems (e.g. the
advantages and drawbacks of different means of distribution, such as
broadcasting, closed circuit, recording, audiovisual copying centres); at the
level of media (courses by newspaper are presumably only one possible
format among many using print; is cinema film entirely irrelevant?; what
are the best applications of sound recording on disc, tape or cassette?); at

the level of teaching method (e.g. the individualization made possible by recording in relation to Learning by Appointment facilities as, sumptuously, in West German videoteles or less grandly, at the Napier College in Edinburgh; or to such independent learning schemes as the Keller Plan; or to Learning Contracts like those negotiated at the Empire State College and elsewhere). This is not just a conventional make-work plea for 'more research'. It is to suggest that the random, spasmodic and chaotic association of the mass media with higher education needs to evolve into something more coherent, nationally and internationally; research — in the sense of R and D — needs to be part of that move to coherence, by being related to the imaginative exploitation of the possibilities for curricula, courses and materials which undoubtedly exist.

References

1. Sir W. Perry, *Open University*, Open University Press, Milton Keynes 1976.
2. Dr J. Scupham, in N. Mackenzie, R. Postgate and J. Scupham, *Open Learning*, Paris, Unesco Press, 1975.
3. Perry, op. cit.
4. Dr A. W. Bates, *Survey of Student Use of Broadcasting, Teaching at a Distance*, 5, pp. 45—52, Open University, Milton Keynes, 1976.
5. Mackenzie *et al.*, op. cit.
6. Professor Dr W. Delva *et al., Wet en Recht*, Brussels, BRT-Open School, 1976.
7. J. Rogers and B. Groombridge, *Right to Learn*, Arrow Books, London, 1976.
8. Mackenzie *et al.*, op. cit.
9. The Open University Charter, para 3.
10. In Mackenzie *et al.*, op cit., p. 348.
11. Open University (1975), Second Submission of the Open University to the Committee on the Future of Broadcasting, Open University, Milton Keynes. A variant of the analysis is included in Mackenzie *et al.*, pp. 60—2.
12. Mackenzie *et al.*, op. cit., p. 348.
13. H. C. Wiltshire, 'Educative into Educational: Television's Transformation', (1963) repro. in A. Rogers (ed.) *The Spirit and the Form*, Department of Adult Education, University of Nottingham, 1976, pp. 47—8.
14. P. Hall, H. Land, R. A. Parker and A. L. Webb, *Change, Choice and Conflict in Social Policy*, Heinemann Educational, London, 1975.
15. See H. C. Wiltshire, 'Teaching through television', in A. Rogers (ed.), op. cit., pp. 50—61.
16. B. Groombridge, 'Adult Education and Broadcasting: Open Education', in A. Rogers (ed.). op. cit., pp. 44—5.
17. *Report of the Committee on Continuing Education* (Venables Report), Open University, Milton Keynes, 1976.
18. Ibid., p. 63.
19. H. C. Wiltshire, op. cit., p. 45.
20. See *Adult Education in Finland*, 13(1) (1976), pp. 16—21.
21. *Adult Education: a Plan for Development*, London, HMSO, 1973.
22. Ibid., p. 88.
23. Rogers and Groombridge, op. cit., pp. 174—5.
24. Ibid., p. 38.
25. Ibid., p. 88.

Part II

Some responses

Chapter 6

Permanent education: a European framework for higher education

J. J. Scheffknecht

Training geared to work emerges as one of the major motive forces for the development of continuing adult education; in particular it is providing the impetus for a nascent system of alternation. In Europe the main features of this trend are:

1. The introduction of laws and occupational agreements which place the right to vocational training on an organized basis.
2. A new definition of the job qualification—training relationship. Both the concept of vocational training as a preparation for one specific job and its opposite, a too general type of training cut off from working life, are coming under the force of criticism as meeting neither the aspirations of individuals nor the imperative needs of the economy.

   The general improvement in the level of training is eliciting qualitative demands on the part of employees as regards how they spend their working hours, which they are less and less inclined to look upon as a parenthesis in their lives. Technological changes entail a constant re-valuing of jobs and the development of economic activities in general is increasingly mirrored in individual or collective re-training. In this context and bearing in mind the present training and job classification systems, the planning of 'human resources' is proving more and more hazardous.
3. A reform of continuing vocational training centred on:
   (a) a change in the methods of analysing 'needs' and information;
   (b) the development of a new system of continuing vocational training: objectives, continuous assessment, alternation, unit/credit systems, 'pédagogie de l'objet technique', diversification of places of training;
   (c) the devising of courses suited to the least qualified workers and those looking for work.
4. A redefinition of the organization of work and life within the firm. Schemes centred on vocational training alone have proved inadequate. There is increasing interest in a reorganization of life in the firm ranging from experiments in new job patterns and the upgrading of manual works to the Scandinavian countries' more comprehensive industrial democracy projects. The effect of the various steps taken in this sphere is to increase the need and opportunity for training. A more fundamental change is, however, the real possibilities they bring for personal development at work.

The right to continuing vocational training and study leave[1]

The laws and agreements in force in the European countries studied set up a system of *continuing* vocational training inasmuch as they recognize, thanks to various arrangements, the right to continuity in the matter of training.

At the same time, they usher in, albeit in a piecemeal fashion, the era of permanent education because they pose the problem of the systematic dovetailing into one another of initial and continuing training.

The general trends noted in the examples studied are as follows:

1. The right of adults to receive education, which is often proclaimed in constitutions is exercised through the right to *study leave*, this being understood to mean a salary or wage-earner's right to participate in training activities during working hours while receiving his salary in full or in part and without risk to his job.

   This concept also covers, rather inadequately, the situation of 'forced leave' experienced by the unemployed, who are entitled to training with a view to resuming work.
2. The schemes are financed by employers, the State or both.
3. Those financed are mainly vocational training schemes or, as yet to a lesser extent certainly, trade union training schemes.
4. Training opportunities are increased and the public authorities are taking a more active part in continuous vocational training. There are many more vocational training instructors and places of training. The objectives and content of training courses are becoming more varied.

The development of continuing vocational training accompanying the tremendous economic growth of the 'sixties underwent intensive institutionalization in the early 'seventies and is suffering today from the slowing down of the economy. The present crisis is, however, causing wage-earners to take notice. Hitherto vocational training has been regarded as a necessary investment on the part of firms to ensure their development; today wage-earners see it as a social guarantee of their security of employment.

Apart from the quantitative and material problems (number of salary earners concerned, training time during paid working hours . . .) the main thing at stake today is that of the power to decide what the objectives, content and methods of training shall be.

Decision-making power in matters of continuing vocational training lies mainly in the hands of employers and of the State. Trade unions are at best consulted.

On the one hand it is essential to keep vocational training linked to the running of the firm and to its particular problems in order to secure the promotion of individual wage-earners. Training is linked to the firm's policy and to employment. On the other hand, the emphasis is placed on mastering work situations, on the struggle against the constraints work imposes and on a more collective, general vocational training conferring multiple skills and enabling workers to at least participate in the general running of the firm.

It is noteworthy that in every country continuing vocational training policy progresses via political and trade union struggles. The differences between the solutions adopted depends of course on the 'cultural' disparities between countries, but above all they are determined by the varying degrees of militancy of the unions, by the liberalism of employers' associations and by the nature of the governments.

New decision-makers — employers and trade unions — have grown up alongside the State with its educational system and the specialist associations and are demanding their full share in the continuing vocational training system. The traditional establishments such as universities are finding themselves in the position of suppliers of services.

Training is ceasing to be the monopoly of training systems — a situation whose full effect on the setting up of a permanent education system is far from being known. Two problems are already emerging clearly today:

1. The right to study leave is only the beginning of a process directed towards securing paid free time for continuing education. We cannot yet forecast what its importance will be in the long term, but it can only increase.

   It is already obvious that the use of this free time cannot be confined to traditional vocational training; it opens up numerous educational possibilities. Study leave will therefore have repercussions on the *whole* education system.
2. Today there are two patterns for these new educational opportunities:
   (a) a system parallel to the traditional one, as favoured in the Federal Republic of Germany, for example.
   (b) a system linked to or dovetailed into initial training, as in France and Italy, for example.

It is clear that the process of transition to a system of permanent education must differ in these two cases.

The job-training relationship: key qualifications, vocational mobility and knowledge

The general organization of vocational training as continuing education alternating with work is accompanied by a more serious crisis regarding its aims and content. Even a superficial examination of the employment market shows that the various manpower problems that arise are mainly caused by the fact that the jobs available increasingly fail to match the skills and qualifications produced by the education system. This situation is exacerbated today by the large number of people seeking employment whose qualifications do not always correspond to the types of job offered. But the employment crisis is only highlighting a pre-existing situation.

Employment problems can no longer be solved either by training geared to a narrow range of occupations or by 'general' education. Nor is an adequate solution to be found in a policy of vocational mobility which consists in manipulating the labour market by moving around manpower trained for adaptability. The simple system of replacing one employee by another with identical training is becoming less and less efficacious.

In this situation the difficulties of forecasting and planning of employment and training in relation to each other are multiplied. A new line of research[2] is tending to break away from the linear job qualification–training relationship. With the mechanistic link between these terms becoming weaker, it is necessary to produce people with skills and qualifications which can be adapted continually to changes in job structures. They must accordingly be qualified differently or even over-qualified. Thus vocational training and general education both find themselves out of favour and a new line of research has been opened up around the concepts of key qualifications and vocational mobility. D. Mertens defines these terms as follows:

Key qualifications are knowledge, aptitudes and skills, which instead of immediate and limited relevance to specific disparate practical activities, confer:

(a) *the ability to perform alternately or simultaneously a wide range of jobs and functions, and*

(b) *the ability to adjust to a series of (largely unforeseeable) changes in the demands made by one's job throughout one's life.*

This line of research may be described briefly as follows: to strike a new balance between employment and training it is necessary to include in the latter knowledge with the widest possible range of different applications, in other words multi-purpose knowledge, which nevertheless at the same time lays the foundation for future retraining.

The subjects taught previously with a view to versatility (the so-called 'general' subjects) are no longer fulfilling their role. We must, therefore, radically revise our ideas of the knowledge likely to fulfil that function in the short, medium and long term. This makes the linear approach, which is, generally speaking, the manpower approach, consisting of projecting the present employment structure into the future and so risking the repetition of the present imbalances, inadequate. The concept of 'occupation' and the current job classifications, it should be remembered, were not established either for forecasting purposes or for educational planners' needs. A person's occupation today is a factor which helps to identify his place in society but in most cases its name does not give an accurate idea of the job performed. Consequently it is vain to hope that better planning will correct the relative irrelevance of the training offered to job requirements.

Many people find work for which they have not been trained. It is, therefore, essential to find out what features of training make such mobility possible and make them an aim of training. This end cannot be achieved either by simply reorganizing the education system in units of training undergone under an alternating or recurrent training scheme, for example, or by merely multiplying 'general' training courses. A balance must be struck between general objectives such as: being capable of mobility, autonomy, critical analysis, etc., and general subjects such as French, Latin, mathematics or accountancy.

The present state of the whole education system is closely bound up with the hierarchy of jobs and the reform of vocational training raises problems for the system as a whole. A redistribution of knowledge is insufficient; in practice it continues to bring about social selection. The effort made, once again under the pressure of the employment situation with all its inherent ambiguities, to redefine education in terms of key qualifications should result in restructuring of knowledge and of the manner of its acquisition.

Other experiments — teaching by operational objectives, centres of interest, technical objects, etc., are directed towards the same goal.

The permanency of vocational training necessitated by the more rapid changes of job structures and made desirable by the growing wishes of individuals for greater freedom in their choice of occupation will bring about not only a reorganization of education but also, and more fundamentally, a questioning of knowledge itself, its division, modes of production, distribution and acquisition. Permanent education will not simply be today's education made permanent: it implies its profound transformation.

The reform of continuing vocational training

Parallel to work on defining a new job-qualification-training relationship and to the negotiations in progress to extend the right and possibilities of access to continuing vocational training, work is being done on the actual practice of training.

Adult education, unlike basic education must always meet adults' real wishes arising out of concrete situations; only then will training be really desired and useful.

A fresh analysis of 'needs' should thus in principle precede every continuing training scheme. Practice, however, is often in conflict with principle:

1. Each of us has training 'needs' which only need to be detected.
2. These needs are either 'conscious', in which case they must be noted down, or 'unconscious', in which case an awareness of them must be created by appropriate methods so that they can then be expressed.

Educationists note, however, that tailor-made courses often come to be modelled very closely on the initial education system:

1. The demand for education increases with the scholastic level of adults: from this it was concluded the people with little schooling had few training 'needs' or were not motivated or scarcely educable. This, incidentally, explained their failure in basic education.
2. Demand is expressed in scholastic terms (e g traditional higher education disciplines, scholastic level).
3. The value of education is seldom perceived other than by reference to

scholastic diplomas and to a social advancement scheme: without any prospect of individual advancement there are no training 'needs'.

In fact, people who talk about 'needs', whether their own or those of others, borrow their responses from the existing educational arsenal: the degree of acculturation to the system is such that the expression of 'individual needs' is only the expression of a social need adopted by the individual as his own. This process is reinforced by the analysis methods used which are conducive to both the functions and the organization of initial training being copied in adult education. It seems that the study of 'needs' is trapped in a vicious circle in which the output after processing the data is exactly the same as the input.

This phenomenon is intensified by the practice of educational institutions which, in order to develop or to protect themselves tend, often unconsciously, to influence the study of 'needs' so that the education supplied very largely determines demand. The result is that the 'needs' expressed by adults often coincide strangely and lastingly with what the institutions have to offer.

Decisions regarding training can be made subject to an examination of these difficulties and carried out, wherever possible, by the people concerned. The advantages are threefold:

1. Training is once again related to all the development problems of a given occupational situation. An analysis of general problems helps to disclose the cause of malfunctioning (organization of work, running, information, giving of orders) which is often too hastily ascribed to individuals' incompetence.

2. Those concerned may thus discover a further interest in training once they comprehend the situation better.

3. Adults can then discuss more easily together how to change their situation and negotiate their training with the educational authorities because they understand better how it serves both individuals and the community.

Such practices throw training open to all categories of staff who see or find no interest in education.

Much is at stake. If training is to serve the interests of adults, their personal development and their emancipation instead of being a disguised means of increasing their alienation (dependence) they *must* already have learned to express their demand for training, for upon that hangs the whole educational process.

Collective advancement schemes

There is a need to integrate in a comprehensive permanent education project collective and individual development activities at present split up and administered under the separate head of health and social work and cultural action. Collective schemes are a radical departure from educational measures designed solely with the individual in mind. Their promoters have seen the failure of individual education as an effective means of combating social inequality, which they claim it has, on the contrary, tended to accentuate.

This re-thinking is the result of the following analysis: educational and cultural inequalities are linked to social inequalities, being the product of social conditions imposed on adults both individually and collectively. They are directly related to the position held by groups within society, to the social class to which they belong and to their geographical situation (built-up or rural areas).

Educational and cultural opportunity is, to a great extent, determined by social position. An egalitarian education given to people of different social classes will not in fact be egalitarian. All the efforts made by an individual to acquire education can change the social position of a minority only slightly; in fact individual social advancement is rarely accompanied by real cultural advancement: 'social parvenus' too often remain culturally underdeveloped.

Today it is clear to anyone who views the situation objectively that education is always a political instrument; it is never free from political bias. To demand its 'neutrality' amounts in fact to making it a conservative instrument.

Educators of adults, cultural animateurs and social workers are exceptionally aware of this situation because the effectiveness of their endeavours is always bounded by the conditions under which adults work, live and relax. These structural obstacles are particularly obvious in educational schemes born of crises, whether they be economic, social, cultural or ecological. In these situations priority is given to collective schemes which seek means of combining personal and collective development and social change. That is why it is often difficult to separate collective schemes from political action, and some educationists do indeed fall into the trap. Most, however, aim at a type of scheme which is not a surrogate of political action and which preserves adults' freedom of choice in that sphere but which, conversely, does not isolate political conditions from social change and personal development.

Tutors and animateurs are striving today to find a justification for their work and to situate it in the right context; many of them voice the complaint, which we must echo, that they are, however, forced to assume a conservative rather than an innovatory role. Political disapproval often weighs upon the schemes which concern us here, for they are, in fact, an integral part of the social struggle, all of whose contradictory features they display. There are, however, some major exceptions to such censure and it is then that the schemes we are now going to describe can be developed.

Community centres and study circles[3]

Community centres

These centres, set up to serve a municipality, district or small region, can most often be defined as places where educational resources are made freely available to residents. Some centres fulfil this function in addition to organizing specific educational activities. They all work on the principle that it is for groups of adults to mobilize themselves to manage their own education, whether for purposes of further training or educational, cultural or community activities.

In these centres, groups of adults may find:

(a) *material resources*: meeting rooms, projection rooms, a theatre, an auditorium, do-it-yourself workshops, craft workshops, a library, documentation, materials for self-teaching, programmed learning, audiovisual equipment, etc.;

(b) *human resources*: an information and guidance post, animateurs for the use of material equipment, technical assistants, etc.

Where these activities are not part of an environmental action plan they almost always encounter the same limitations: they presuppose a stock-taking of social, educational and cultural problems already solved and thus call for individuals and groups who have already mobilized or organized themselves and who have a clear idea of what education can be expected to achieve. The result is that despite their intentions these centres continue to be selective and the people who use them belong mainly to the social classes already privileged in the matter of education, employment and leisure. It is true that a minority of 'militants' can be found in these centres, which can thus play a part in producing the various agents of change, though that is only a secondary role.

It is clearly important to site and develop such centres judiciously, but that is not enough alone, since precisely the most economically, socially and educationally deprived social categories are in a great measure excluded from them. It is becoming increasingly clear that the transition from a system of scholastic and selective education to the self-management of educational objectives and resources will not occur spontaneously and that it must be organized. Some centres are already working along these lines.

Study circles

It would be entirely wrong to consider study circles purely from the aspect of the organization of training activities and of their educational value, which is, however, undeniable. They have long represented, much more basically, a substantial and original opportunity for collective advancement at national level. Through them, the State finances the free organization by citizens and their organizations (associations, trade unions, political parties, churches) of any educational activity which brings together a sufficient number of people to justify the existence of a study group. A vast free educational service is thus made operational. The only restriction imposed by the State is administrative (number of people per group, educational content, duration, quality of the teaching and leadership).

The originality of this system lies in the fact that the groups of adults concerned are given the material means of acquiring the knowledge which they feel they need. Annual attendance figures show the impact of study circles at municipal level. The quality of working democracy at local and national level is often ascribed in part to them.

Study circles do, however, have their limitations:

(a) the difficulty of reaching the most deprived sections of society;
(b) the difficulty of applying what has been learned to everyday situations (Norway and Sweden).

Collective training schemes[4]

These schemes have all grown out of the same socio-economic context and have roughly the same aims.

An economic crisis hits an area which provides many people with employment but which is heavily dependent on one branch of industry. Production is slowed down or stopped. Working hours are reduced. There is immediate or foreseeable unemployment. Training is required which permits a change of job which might entail geographical mobility not only for the employee but also for his family. Thus a whole population finds itself in a situation which education can help to remedy both at individual and at community level by raising the general cultural and educational level so as to enable the region to adapt, providing opportunities for re-training and for general training of a nature to facilitate occupational mobility, encouraging a constructive attitude to the economic situation, promoting collective action to restore job opportunities, etc.

An 'intervening' body which takes charge of the scheme with a view to placing it on its own feet

The basic educational principle which guides all the work of the 'intervening' body is that of enabling the people and machinery concerned to run the scheme themselves. By defining its educational action as 'intervention', this body seeks to avoid as far as possible a relationship of dependency and to make sure that the group becomes involved in a process of self-education and of running the training scheme themselves. The 'intervening' body's action is concerned with giving a general lead to the scheme and is characterized by the following stages:

1. The setting up within a community of structures to analyse the demand for training and the community's expectations as regards adult education: rather than taking over from the parties concerned and/or the community, the 'intervening' body provides them with the means, methods and material to work out their own educational response to their real needs;
2. A proposal to set up a policy-making body representative of the social

forces in the community (public authorities, employers, workers, administrative bodies, consumer associations) to be in charge of the scheme followed by the withdrawal of the 'intervening' body into the background to allow the scheme to stand on its own feet;

3. The development thereby of training close to the places where training problems exist, that is to say in the places where the organized life of the community goes on.

Upward evaluation of the objectives and content of education, usually regarded as of secondary importance because they are far from the academic disciplines and the accepted image of scholastic learning.

This covers everything coming under the heading of 'general' education but which should be described as '*methodological*' training: development of spoken and written expression, examination of problems, analysis of cases and of situations, learning of individual and group work methods; in short, all the methodological processes which permit the transfer and use of knowledge and methods learned *for the purposes and in the context of daily life*. A methodological training of this kind tends in the direction of a *global concept* of education.

Education by objectives negotiated by all the social partners and organized in a unit/credit system

Education by reference to objectives is particularly important in collective education because once it is decided that a scheme is to be a collective one, and thus closely matched to the needs and aspirations of the whole community, the community must be permitted to define its own objectives. This process will, moreover, enable the community to keep a permanent check on the work of their teachers by analysing the results of the scheme in the light of progress made towards the objectives. This is a departure from scholastic education because it makes possible real participation by the students and opens the way to the acquisition of knowledge by a whole community.

Tutors from the community trained in the community

Collective schemes endeavour, wherever possible, to use teachers with the same background as the students on the basis that those who know more can contribute to the education of those who know less. This policy rests on the following analysis: every community possesses its own social and ideological values which distinguish it from other communities; schools and institutions of higher education, however, do not take account of these differences and their teachers are, by definition, interchangeable and able to adapt to any public.

As the aim of a collective scheme is precisely to concentrate on the particular development problems of a given community, it tries, on the contrary, to rely on teachers from the community and to train them in the community so as to reduce the risk of irrelevancy and reinforce the community's will to assume responsibility for all the objectives of the training scheme. These people are not necessarily professional teachers; on the contrary, all potential educators are called upon.

It then becomes possible to develop a teaching method which is based on familiar and concrete experience, which introduces centres of interest closely linked to daily life and which is applicable to the acquisition of scientific and technical knowledge, the power of expression and initiation into the cultural and economic world.

The 'intervening' body takes over the training of these teachers, at least at the outset.

Community development and cultural advancement schemes[5]

The distinction between these collective training schemes might seem artificial as they both have the same aim: to promote collective advancement through educational action geared to the organizational and operational structures — economic, social, cultural, educational and medical — of the community concerned. However, because of the special circumstances surrounding them, collective schemes emphasize educational aspects rather than social and cultural problems. They aim at the advancement of a community by means of vast improvement in its general standard of education.

General characteristics

These schemes are designed for a specific social group or community and are always confined to a restricted geographical area. They are organized to meet a latent or acute crisis: serious unemployment, cultural and educational underdevelopment, concentration of 'underprivileged' persons in an urban area, rural underdevelopment, affirmation of a cultural identity, etc.

The main characteristics of these *situations* are as follows:

1. Incomes lower than the national average, high level of unemployment, economic dependence on the State (various social welfare allowances).
2. Poor health record with a particularly high infant mortality rate, poor housing and sanitary conditions, overpopulation, juvenile delinquency, level of education below the national average, little cultural activity, unrewarding occupations, night shifts, etc.

We might add some characteristics peculiar to the rural environment:

3. Distance, isolation, depopulation, emigration.
4. Few educational and cultural facilities.

By means of the community development scheme, it is sought:

(a) to identify the social problems in all their forms;

(b) to take steps to solve them or incite those concerned to solve them;

(c) to back up social action by educational action;

(d) to encourage the members of the community to *participate* as far as possible in the scheme by defining their needs, problems and aspirations, by suggesting measures and by helping to put them into practice.

The general objectives are:

(a) to improve the quality of individual, family and community life;

(b) to extend the range of economic and social opportunities;

(c) to develop individuals and in the community a capacity to create or seize opportunities to improve their well-being.

These schemes therefore amount to more than social assistance which, in the long term, confirms and organizes these groups in their marginality by creating, in urban areas, positive pockets of outcasts. The community scheme aims to replace the passivity these situations engender by an active attitude and a capacity for collective action to remedy their causes.

The very way in which such schemes are conducted is designed to set an example in this respect: it is sought to avoid social assistance being accompanied by educational assistance, which would be equally alienating; residents are therefore invited to contribute to the analysis of difficulties and problems, the identification of needs, the choice of solutions and operational methods, the management of resources, etc.

Educational action is thus built into a far more comprehensive programme calling on the services of a wide range of authorities: child welfare, health and social welfare, social security, housing, employment, police, the local council, employers' and workers' organizations, churches.

Educational action proper is exploring new paths since it is chiefly concerned with social groups already rejected by the education system and having consequently little desire to return to traditional forms: if they were useless in the past, why should they be any better now?

The specifically educational side of the scheme may be defined as follows:

1. Organization of collective expression and demands where education is concerned.
2. The formation of the various parties involved into an intervention team to establish a close working relationship with the population.
3. The mounting of other activities as a complement to educational schemes:
   (a) integrated as far as possible with the analysis of problems or with case studies; and
   (b) concentrating on matters of social, economic and political importance to the residents.

The main task is to establish a system of priorities for these activities which corresponds to the population's requirements.

Here is an example of a breakdown of one scheme:

1. Information on social rights, information centre manned by residents, setting up of tenants' and residents' associations, organization and running of crèches, day nurseries, courses on the organization and conducting of meetings (minute-writing, agenda, introduction, summing-up).
2. Adult literacy, catching up of schooling missed (lower and upper secondary level).
3. Shorthand-typing, cooking, dress-making, domestic economy, drawing, woodwork, gymnastics, swimming, reading, theatrical production, etc.

And in the case of a rural scheme:

4. Improvement of traditional activities, introduction of new activities in conjunction with the development plan: animal husbandry, flower-growing, wine-growing, agricultural mechanization, use of fertilizers, marketing of products, setting up of cooperatives, local handicraft production, reception of tourists, provision of accommodation, foreign languages, musical groups, brass bands, folk dancing, etc.
5. Training in the management of local affairs, civic education, trade-union education, political education.

It is always sought to fit the various activities into a concerted development plan rather than allow them to be carried on as parallel schemes superimposed on the population. They are founded on the principle of the decentralization of initiative and management and they call for participation or self-management.

Principles underlying organization

1. All the residents of an area or region to be regarded as concerned.
2. Their economic and social problems to be the starting point of the scheme.
3. The educational approach to be a global one, i.e. embracing problems of vocational training and/or general education, basic education, cultural education and animation, training to cope with the ordinary problems of life (family, work, community), etc.
4. Educational needs to be made articulate.
5. The political side to be given priority over the strictly educational side and the organization of community action to be encouraged.
6. Representatives of the residents to be given overall political responsibility for the scheme.
7. The everyday running of the scheme to be in the hands of representatives of the local population.
8. Flexibly managed training and animation centres to be set up.
9. Modern technical media to be used and mobile teaching units to be introduced.
10. Full-time animateurs to be trained and employed; at the same time generous use to be made of part-time animateurs.

11. Traditional channels of education to be associated with the scheme and used; a technical and scientific body to be available for the purposes of coordination, advice and evaluation.
12. The scheme to be conducted in the public service framework.
13. Laws and regulations to be introduced to ensure its adequate duration, etc.

Conclusion

Whereas individual advancement schemes seek to reduce educational and cultural inequalities, collective advancement schemes try to act on the social framework by means of individual and collective education.

The process of collective advancement arose from the recognition that educational, cultural and social inequality are closely interdependent, but the accent is placed on their economic causes and their class correlations.

Such schemes are feeling their way towards global development strategy which covers all the problems encountered by the various social groups within a given geographical area and is designed to benefit the mass of the people and not just the elite. In fact, this move towards global action is meeting with structural obstacles.

Deep institutional dividing lines keep the machinery for cultural action, social action and educational action in quite separate compartments. However, in everyday practice, cultural animateurs, social workers and educators are becoming less and less able to live with this division which impairs their efficiency and interferes with development possibilities of the individuals and communities concerned.

One fact must be noted here: as each of these fields of activity tends to encroach on one of the others or to use its techniques, it lays itself or finds itself laid open to challenge. Thus:

1. The principles of the democratization of the cultural heritage come up against plans for cultural democracy; the dissemination of culture and cultural animation come into conflict with cultural action; questions are asked about the role and action of cultural animateurs in society and about their training for the task of integration.
2. Social workers discover the limitations of social assistance; their action in the long-run institutionalizes the marginality of the so-called under-privileged rather than aiding their social reintegration; they no longer wish to salve the conscience of a growth-orientated society which is sacrificing a section of its population.
3. Education's function as the perpetuator of the existing social organization is denounced, the mere passing on of a body of knowledge is rejected and the political and technical function of the educator is once more called into question.

Moreover, there is a growing wish to unmask the political function inherent in cultural, social and educational schemes, to play an openly acknowledged role in creating an awareness of the conditions really required for personal development and to combat alienation, in all its forms by education.

It is against this background that these spheres of activity are reviewing their plans today, all three of them with an eye to permanent education, which is emerging as a unifying myth and beginning to take on a clearer form. Today we must recognize their limits. Social change stems from political action: collective schemes can induce political action, they cannot direct it.

Political training schemes

There is a political function inherent in any educational activity. It is obvious that the relationship between education and politics is central to any discussion of permanent education: the relationship between the ruling political power and the system of permanent education is thus crucial. The various models we shall propose for the future of education will depend primarily on that relationship, the pedagogical aspects remaining secondary.

Two experiments provide models differing greatly in their approach to political education inasmuch as the societies they propose are different.

A political and civic training

The Burgenland experiment in Austria
The aim of this regional scheme is to set up a network of political training centres for the permanent local representatives of political parties, trade union officials, municipal councillors and citizens interested in this form of political education. The task of this network is to raise the level of political awareness, to develop more active and more critical attitudes to the social environment and to develop an understanding of democracy among participants.

The training consists of a basic general political education (modern history, political science and economics, a study of the constitution, administration, public speaking, local politics, sociology, psychology) linked to the examination of local, national and international issues. It takes as its basis the social environment of each individual and endeavours to awaken a political consciousness which is both constructive and critical, so that each person can take a more active part in public responsibilities and decision-making.

A certificate is awarded on completion of the course, which is recommended by two main parties — the Socialist Party and the People's Party — to their full-time officials and militants. The curriculum is arranged in unit/credits and progress is assessed by tests and examinations. The scholastic nature of the course is deliberate and is justified by the fact that it is designed primarily for sections of the population (manual and office workers, farm labourers, civil servants, small farmers, craftsmen) who require a well-structured framework in which to learn. That is why the break with traditional schooling methods must be gradual and slow. Greater social independence must, paradoxically, be attained through dependence on a school system.

The teachers are academics who try to hand over to former students from their courses.

The scheme, which reaches a large percentage of the population (3 per cent to 5 per cent in some places) is directed jointly by the two big rival national parties. This collaboration is made possible by:

(a) the fact that neither party questions the liberal organization of society and that both are agreed on the necessity for reform;
(b) their agreement on a basic training in 'general politics', the use made of which at local and national levels remains in the hands of the parties and their internal machinery;
(c) their common wish to accustom politicians to tolerance and dialogue.

The scheme obviously affords possibilities of individual advancement to full-time party officials, trade union officials and local councillors. It seems to have a real effect on the running of the respective institutions but it is too early to judge its collective impact on local or regional political life. It is true that this education is relatively uncritical, but in that respect it is in keeping with the prevailing political trend in Austria. But at the same time it is very remarkable that a scheme offering civic and political education in a free, pluralist context on such a scale can be carried out in the normal adult education institutional framework.

A critical political training

The counter-school project of ISCO

The Institut Supérieur de Culture Ouvrière (ISCO) was set up in 1962 by the Belgian Mouvement Ouvrier Chrétien (MOC). Its general aim is to work for the cultural, social and political advancement of men and women. Its more specific aim is to train a future elite of workers as animateurs. It is a *functional* body, that is to say it receives its political instructions from the MOC.

The experiment which we are now going to describe differs radically from all those we have described to date:

1. It is explicitly designed to further the social and political conflict and is organically linked to a political movement which disputes the established social order.
2. It seeks, through education, to help to transfer power to other hands.
3. It challenges not only the ruling economic power but also the educational and cultural structures that serve its ends.
4. It trains militants, agents of change, and to do so it is developing a type of education tailored to the society it hopes to establish; it is proposing counter model for education, in fact a counter-school.

The training scheme is directed expressly towards transforming society and is addressed primarily to men and women who are already committed to economic, social, political, missionary, educational or cultural work or the like or who are on the point of undertaking such work. It is sought by this means to strengthen their possibilities of action in the various situations in which they operate: trade union delegations, socio-educational teams, political groups, church communities, neighbourhood associations, cultural centres, urban recreation centres, school councils, parents' associations, peace movements, movements of aid to the Third World, etc.

The Institute's course presupposed the acquisition of basic training in the local union groups. The scheme thus provides supplementary training designed to increase the action and mobilization potential of militants. Trainees are selected on the basis of their capacity to act and not of the level of their academic knowledge. The selection procedure tries to minimize as far as possible the risk of giving long, expensive training to people who would not use what they had learned in subsequent campaigns.

The Institute's priorities are:

1. To provide training and further training for full-time union workers, members of political parties and social or socio-cultural activists working in various militant situations, so as to improve their intellectual capacity and their ability to act effectively in a given situation.
2. To train animateurs or politically-minded citizens for political action and cultural animation with a view to the active and purposeful use of leisure. The idea is to give adults an introductory training enabling them to play an active part in the democratic transformation of society within the municipality, school, cultural centre, neighbourhood association, base community, family, etc.
3. To try to supply all activists with the essential means of analysing society from the political, economic, social and cultural points of view and so understanding its structure, challenging it and taking steps to change and reform it.

Activists' training is based on a critical analysis of traditional education. The two main points of this analysis are as follows: first, traditional education is conservative. By ignoring or completely avoiding political, social and cultural education it prevents citizens from understanding their present political and social situation and in no way encourages them to work to change it. Although higher education is gradually becoming more accessible, it is still the preserve of the already privileged social classes. Working-class children are obliged to receive the traditional neoliberal-inspired education which presents an undoubted risk of tinging their ideology and culture.

Second, traditional education is based on technocratic principles and acts as a nursery for technicians at all levels who in turn reinforce the rigid hierarchy of the social system. Education is diverted to serve the interests of a capitalist minority and the purposes of the established order.

In the light of this analysis a current is emerging in favour of an efficient system of permanent education devised for adults with their help, taking as its starting point the problems of their everyday life and work and aiming at the transformation of society. A counter-school scheme is being worked out gradually in opposition to the selective, elitist, competitive, individualistic, hierarchical and authoritarian education of the traditional system. ISCO has set up an educational network which is attuned in both its general organization and its teaching approach to the political aims outlined.

Organization and functioning of the training system

The whole scheme is founded on the greatest possible decentralization of initiative and on the wish to progress gradually to self-management.
There are three levels of organization:

1. National;
2. Regional;
3. Local: class-group and sub-groups.

The class-group situation is central to the scheme for it is here that decentralization and self-management are put into practice.

1. National level

It is at this level that educational measures are coordinated with political and social measures, that aims are redefined and training programmes finally adopted. A small group of permanent staff of the Institute plus an 'intervention' team is in charge of the scheme. Its main task is to ensure that the system does not become bureaucratic and that the rank and file are always able to express their viewpoint.

It is responsible for training tutors and for general administration.

2. Regional level

Regional centres are born of regional demand and requirements; there are twenty throughout the country. They constitute a liaison:

(a) between groups of students and the various regional organizations;
(b) between the region and the central body: their delegates assist in the formulation of national policy. The following matters are handled primarily at this level:
    (i)   student recruitment policy and methods;
    (ii) social and ideological guidance of teachers and animateurs;
    (iii) involvement of animateurs and students in the political, social, and cultural conflicts of the region, etc.

3. Local level

(a) *The class-group*   This is where the teaching is done. The class which is held on Saturday comprises at least thirty people who are on a four-year course. The course is highly organized and is in great demand.

(b) The class council   The class council is vested with authority over teaching matters. It comprises all the students, teachers and representatives of MOC bodies at regional and national level. This is where criticism is voiced of the course in general and in detail and where students' and teachers' work is assessed. Future teachers come here to submit and defend their proposals. The critical analysis concerns not only teaching problems but also the ideological nature of the course. The relevance of a class on economics as opposed to a class on sociology, the ability of a particular animateur, the relative importance of a course on Marxist economics as compared with liberal economics, the unjustified absence of certain militants from courses, etc., are all discussed by the council.

(c) Sub-groups   Each class is sub-divided into groups of four to six people. Students must meet once a week in one of these. They meet at members' homes and their purpose is twofold:

(i) to serve as a place for the revision of classwork and for practical work;
(ii) to provide mutual methodological and psychological assistance and give an opportunity to compare and contrast training and action.

The didactic programme

As we have already stressed, it is not a matter of training specialists or of passing on a particular body of knowledge but of promoting the intellectual, methodological and critical faculties of activists. The following priorities where teaching methods are concerned derive from that choice.

Priority to a practical approach and to active methods

Adult education with a view to social action must find a method which bridges the gap between experience and theory. A theoretical introduction to the various spheres of social, political and cultural action must keep in close touch with the realities of the modern world and with the social practices of the worker-students. It must be based on the contradictions of life as experienced and on knowledge already acquired. The general method is an active one, passing through the following stages:

(a) description and analysis of a situation;
(b) analysis of systems of representation and creation of an awareness of the ideological arguments;
(c) classification of information according to criteria discussed or worked out by the group;
(d) verification of the soundness of the reasoning by testing it against real problems suggested by the group;
(e) organisation and evaluation;
(f) strengthening of the theoretical mastery of situations.

It must be borne in mind that every group of students possesses, thanks to its social experience, knowledge of its own which differs from that of the 'experts'. Neither set of knowledge is sufficient by itself. The important thing is to establish a dialectic relationship between the group's knowledge, which is largely the result of reflecting on practice, and the knowledge of specialists in a given discipline. The group then generates its own knowledge. In this process, it is sought in particular:

(a) to impart an understanding of the social and political environment by concentrating on the instruments of observation, analysis and information processing rather than supplying ready-made solutions;
(b) to lend more weight to the spontaneous knowledge and suggestions of groups in the face of the highly specialized knowledge of experts.

The whole process is directed towards the acquisition of *knowledge translated into action.*

Priority to a comprehensive critical approach

The individual's introduction to sociology, economics, political science, history and culture is designed to give him an overall picture that will enable him to understand and analyse the relationships between the various mechanisms of society so that he can situate himself better in it and so derive guidance for his action. This approach calls for a critical watch on the ideological content of courses, the ideological function of the division of knowledge into disciplines, subjects, etc. It presupposes collaboration among tutors and between tutors and students; the approach is primarily one of synthesis rather than of analysis.

Priority to expression and articulation

'Taking the floor is the first step towards taking power.'

By learning how to express and state their ideas a group acquires greater independence and develops its creativity. The militant learns to analyse situations and *to live them differently.* He will approach with greater scepticism certain stereotyped views and the apparent logic behind certain social practices. There is likely to be a divergence in language and in the perception of things between himself and others, himself and his family, his working environment and the various communities to which he belongs. Personal equilibrium can be re-established only through social action.

Priority to action-orientated training

Training slanted first and foremost towards social change presupposes not only knowledge and up-to-date methods of learning but also a close link between training and political, social and cultural movements.

The aims we have just described can be achieved only if the teaching system observes the following principles:

Self-management

The assumption of responsibility for their education by the groups themselves is now accepted as basic. The transition from a system which transmits knowledge to one of self-managed collective learning calls for the gradual, methodical replacement of the old precepts, methods and examinations by a new order worked out and lived out by the group.

Self-management requires first and foremost that the course should be planned and conducted at local level and that the acquisition of knowledge translatable into action should be able to rely on the pooling of experience, resources, arguments and collective work by the members of the group. The whole success of this form of collective learning is jeopardized in groups where members do not attend regularly or do not commit themselves fully. Recourse to personalized training methods (correspondence courses, courses suited to individual requirements, unit/credit systems) conflict with or seriously hinder the collective approach.

Whereas the sub-groups are the best place for the self-management of learning, the class council is the place where the rules for self-managed training are worked out and where educational authority lies; it is here that the aims, content and methods of training are discussed and that the quality of the knowledge gained by groups, sub-groups and individuals is assessed. Here too the conditions for the renewal of the contracts of animateurs are decided.

As collective training in practice requires that students maintain a high level of attendance at all activities, it seems logical to impose the same requirements on animateurs as regards their presence at class councils, meetings of animateurs, retraining sessions and group discussions.

Formative and constant evaluation

All the possibilities described above are meaningful only if there is a willingness to measure their effectiveness on a continuous basis. In traditional education the competitive examination has always constituted the sole criterion and its selective function has proved very efficient. To conclude from this that in a counter-system, any assessment of knowledge acquired must be banned would be sheer demagogy.

In the traditional education system the purpose of assessment can only be to establish the validity of the knowledge acquired by comparison with a standard. Assessment is therefore a judgement made after training and in no way forms part of it. Selection weeds out those who have been unable faithfully to reproduce the standard responses, the officially sanctioned knowledge, inculcated. In a self-managed project, evaluation is a *constant constituent part of the learning process.* Learning to master a tool is synonymous with knowing, at a given moment, one's capacity to use it.

As the transition is made from individual education to collective learning, it is essential for the whole group constantly to check its progress. Bearing that in mind, *collective assessments* normally reflect the quality of *collective work.* The criteria for collective assessment must be determined by the whole group, students and animateurs alike. For a collective mark to be given unilaterally by the animateur would not make sense and would deprive the group of one of the dimensions of its training. Collective assessment must not, however, rule out an *individual check on the knowledge acquired and efforts made by each person.* The group must analyse any excessive differences between its members and take the necessary steps to correct them, in particular by mutual help.

This process operates through the *discussions* generally held by every sub-group, in which both students and animateurs take part on an equal footing. In this way it is possible to judge the standards which self-managed groups set themselves and to regulate the relationship between educational and militant action.

Conclusion

Éducation permanente is not an idea which has to be snatched from utopia; the seeds of it can be found in the present educative and cultural processes of which we must clarify the exact nature and the prime function, the qualities and the limitations, the myths and the contradictions. It is in the analysis of the present that we find the reasons for a fragmented adult education system, marginal and underused, tied to economic growth and the social hierarchy, essentially for the upper and middle classes.

It is equally from an analysis of the present situation that we can elicit the requirements of a different educational plan.

At the next stage of our work we shall analyse the further implications of *éducation permanente.* For the present, however, some preliminary conclusions:

1. *Éducation permanente* and the extended schooling

The major trap to be avoided by *éducation permanente* is that of permanent schooling. A very close relationship has progressively become established between prolonged educational opportunity and prolonged schooling.

School would be the place for personal development; the school system which is very hierarchical and bureaucratic sets itself up as the instrument of socialization and equal opportunities. In reality it continues to function as a system for the selection of elites and the legitimizing of their political power and social prestige as just recompense for their superior abilities.

'The school system grades people and in so doing degrades them.' Those who are degraded are forced to accept their level of attainment and the position it gives them in the social system, as a proper consequence of their supposed intellectual and cultural inferiority. The social pyramid and the educational pyramid are superimposed upon and reinforce each other. the school system serves that of social discrimination. By seizing the educative role without being able properly to fulfil it, it paradoxically works towards the educational and cultural impoverishment of the majority of people.

We are not saying that professional training in a college of technical education, for example, cannot benefit those who follow it or that it is not to some extent an emancipating experience; but we are forced to state that, but for a few exceptions, those who follow such courses join the ranks of unskilled workers. Their only opportunity for personal development is often lost as a result of the realization of their social and educational alienation.

These ideas are not new but when a framework for *éducation permanente* is developing and when continuing education for adults is establishing itself along the lines of initial training, should we not clarify what is at stake; what are we in the process of making permanent?

We find ourselves facing the following alternatives:

1. To construct an alternating school system, a *recurrent education* which consists above all of reorganizing present syllabuses and marrying them to the cycle of life, particularly people's working life.

   This view of *permanent schooling* is one of the major reference points to which the plan for *éducation permanente* is attaching itself. It consists firstly of recognizing that the prime function of the school systems is a selective process giving access to the work and power hierarchies. The function of such a system would be above all the mimicking of an unequal social organization: it would be a tool of social integration.

2. To promote a concrete and continuing possibility of personal development making use of the whole range of educational and cultural methods at school and in everyday life for the benefit of the greatest number of people.

   This view of the *permanence of personal development* constitutes the second reference point of *éducation permanente*. It assumes that the obstacles which hinder its realization at the level of social organization are removed; it involves the idea of a society with no hierarchical structure where the quality of everyday life is restored to its rightful place and where productivity would no longer be the sole criterion.

But these changes cannot be considered as so many preliminaries; if the continuing education of adults should primarily serve towards the reduction of alienating influences and of everything which diminishes individuals and social groups, then it should be at the centre of every struggle against these alienating influences. *Éducation permanente* will then be a tool for social emancipation, a global and critical educational approach to everyday life.

This alternative emerges very clearly from the mass of contradictions which characterize the present situation in the continuing education of adults which we have been studying.

These same studies show that the overriding tendency today goes rather towards 'continuous schooling' in adult education and even further, towards the same thing in the whole of *éducation permanente*.

2. *Éducation permanente* and the social crisis

The idea of *éducation permanente* was formulated in a period of rapid growth in the industrially developed countries.

The strong growth of the link between production and consumption, and the policy of developing products and technologies have brought in their train a similar policy of bringing up to date and renewing knowledge at a time when the whole educational system is being questioned. This is the general context into which were born, during the 'sixties and early 'seventies, the various acts and agreements on continuing professional training, accompanied by notions of recurrence or permanence in education.

Intellectual activity or, simply, professional knowhow became the important factors in the re-training of the work-force. In return, the highering of the standard of living and the relative increase in free time, have developed individual and collective aspirations towards increased knowledge and towards an enriched living and working environment. But at the same time, alongside those who have benefited, there accumulate those excluded from this growth; young people and women seeking work or professional qualifications, the unemployed, immigrants, prisoners, delinquents, those living in rural areas, artisans and small shopkeepers.

At a time when continuing education finds itself mobilized in the service of economic growth and for the benefit of its privileged participants (the upper classes, middle classes, and working class elites) it also finds itself being asked to diminish or hide the abuses of this same economic growth; education becomes at one and the same time an agent of growth and social assistance.

It is true also, and we noted their importance right at the beginning of our studies, that educational and cultural activities were developing which were deeply at odds with official policies: competing courses, paraeducational activities, collective and community activities, self-managed educational activities, 'pirate' schools and radio, street theatre . . . Marginal activities or the germs of a serious educational and cultural renewal? In any case it was in this very general context, where economic considerations constituted the principal means of educational development, that the Council of Europe's idea of '*éducation permanente*' was born and that the study of pilot experiments touched on here have taken place. They all reflect an economic situation determined within the framework of defined social systems.

Is this situation still the same at the time of writing? Is the economic crisis through which we are passing not putting seriously in question our economic and social order and particularly what appeared to be an inevitable evolution towards *éducation permanente*?

However, the economic crisis is accompanied by a feeling of weariness towards a situation of unregulated economic growth.

The issues of May 1968 rise from history to find new relevance; the demand for the right to work is accompanied by concern about the quality of such work, the seeking after social betterment takes second place to preoccupations about the quality of life, and ecological movements become a political force.

Is this a passing trend or a deep change? It is up to the social citizens to reply.

We will say that it is perhaps paradoxically in a new economic and social future thus opened that *éducation permanente* will find its real opportunity and true dimension.

It will in any case be indispensable in the construction of such a future.

The editors wish to thank Mr W. Toynbee for translating part of this chapter.

References and notes

1. Examples were studied in France, Federal Republic of Germany, Italy, Norway and Sweden.
2. Cf. Mertens: *Key qualifications in basic and further education*, Council of Europe, CCC/EES (72) 110.
3. For example: Residential colleges, Scandinavia; Villeneuve experiment, France; Community colleges, university extra-mural centres, United Kingdom; People's universities, Netherlands and Federal Republic of Germany.
4. Information based on the Merlebach collective training scheme (ACUCES). Six experiments of this type are at present being conducted in France.
5. Schemes visited include: cultural and community development scheme in Bari, Italy; community development scheme in the Swiss Jura; permanent education scheme in La Rochelle, France; 'Télé-Promotion Rurale' in France; community development scheme in Liverpool, UK; and adult education schools in the Netherlands.

Further reading

J. J. Scheffknecht, *Permanent Education and Society*, Council of Europe, Strasbourg, 1976.

J. J. Scheffknecht, *Work of Consolidation of the Evaluation of Pilot Experiments in the Permanent Education Field*, Council of Europe, Strasbourg, 1977.

Chapter 7

The independent alternative

Professor Max Beloff

I was originally asked to write this chapter specifically about the University College at Buckingham but I have preferred the more general theme indicated by its title. The main reason is a general philosophical one. The more one studies the history of institutions and especially of educational institutions, the more clear it becomes that no founding fathers however precise their aims and the rules they originally lay down can hope to control the development of the institution they create. Unless it collapses and dies, it will develop a life and momentum of its own which cannot be foreseen. It may come into existence as a response to a particular pressure and be altered so as to meet quite different needs. I have in my time been a member of five Oxford colleges, three of ancient and two of recent creation. Not a single one of them would now conform in what it does to what its founders intended; though particular elements do of course survive from the original conception. Or again, if one takes the story of Buckingham's slightly senior academic neighbour, the Open University, it is already clear that its role is not precisely what it was in the mind of Jennie Lee or Harold Wilson when it was founded.

Writing as Buckingham is at the end of its first year of operation, it is already clear that the problems it has thrown up and the opportunities it offers include many that the original planning board assembled in the late 'sixties did not foresee and perhaps could not have foreseen. I suspect that by the time this chapter is in print the mere fact of growth in a second year of operation will have made further demands upon our capacity for improvization.

Another general point is that while one can safely set out one's individual views about a general question such as the role of the State in higher education, to deal with a particular institution from inside it runs the risk of distorting the picture in accordance with one's own angle of vision or mere prejudice. All institutions function in ways that represent some kind of consensus between those responsible for running them, and what they actually do may not wholly reflect the wishes of any single individual. When it is a matter of stating their underlying assumptions it is even more dangerous for one person among those involved to claim the right to speak for all.

I believe that these arguments apply with particular force to the case of Buckingham since the reasons that led to its establishment were themselves the product of a number of currents in the thinking of the 'sixties that led to the call for setting up an 'Independent University' while the ultimate decision to go ahead with what it was decided to call 'The University College at Buckingham' was the product of quite particular circumstances. While the definition of 'independence' to mean not in receipt of a government block grant through the Universities Grants Committee (UGC) was arrived at fairly early on, the other aspects of independence were only hammered out in the course of experience.[1] Some decisions were arrived at with relative ease; not to recruit students through the Universities Central Council on Admissions (UCCA) machinery but actively to seek discretionary grants for those admitted; to seek membership of the FSSU and USS pension schemes; not to be involved in the financing of student union activities through the compulsory allocation of a part of the student fees. But other and perhaps equally important decisions about the definition of independence, particularly on the academic side, were more or less forced upon us by the reactions of external bodies.

The decision to award degrees independently of any other body (and to call them 'licences' in the interim before applying for a Royal Charter) was not originally in the minds of the project's initiators. At least three other possibilities were explored; an arrangement with London University as part of its 'external degree' operation; a specific quasi-federal link with another university in Britain or the Commonwealth; and the award of Council for National Academic Awards (CNAA) degrees. For a variety of reasons all these alleys proved blind ones, though it could be argued that at a very considerable sacrifice of parts of the original plan something might have been worked out with the CNAA, if it had been financially and humanly possible to delay the opening date by a year or two.

What is quite clear is that had any one of these possibilities materialized, the degree of 'independence' the College enjoyed would have been very significantly less than it is now. It could indeed be argued − and I personally would subscribe to this view − that the degree of independence would for practical purposes have been so limited to the mere financial aspect that it is doubtful whether the enterprise would have been worth embarking upon at all from an academic point of view. It is equally true that if we had limited ourselves, as some people would have preferred, to a broad general education at the undergraduate level and had therefore not included law among our original offerings, the 'recognition' of the licence as an acceptable substitute for BA or LLB degree by the Council for Legal Education and the Law Society which was the real breakthrough in the College's fortunes would not have been available, and that the favourable disposition of the universities towards the licence as an entry qualification for postgraduate studies would not itself have been sufficient to enable us to get off the ground. Or again, one could say that the existence of a convention about external examiners which is well understood in this country but not in many others, provided a solution for monitoring standards without recourse to State action which elsewhere would not have been so easily available.

One could say then, that the run-up years and the first year of operation have been largely devoted in one sense to the task of working out what is meant by 'independence' in this context. The word 'alternative' is perhaps equally ambiguous but can be dealt with more succinctly. It is here that the note of caution as to personal bias comes in. I happen to believe that there is a good case for saying that the State should never be the principal provider of education at any level, and that its role should be as far as possible restricted to financial subventions of voluntary effort with the minimum of direct intervention. On the other hand, I believe equally strongly that one must work with what one has inherited from the past and that utopianism is essentially unproductive and even boring. I can see no possibility that in a country where the State finances higher education to the overwhelming extent that it does in Britain (and indeed almost every-where except in the United States) an independent sector could develop in the way in which one exists (greatly to the nation's benefit) in primary and secondary education. By an 'independent alternative', I mean merely that the existence of one independent institution could be the means of calling into question some of the assumptions of the existing system, both on the financial-administrative side and in academic matters, and that by so doing it might affect the way in which things were done in the State system.

It would of course be a more important and more impressive experi-ment if there had been the resources available to contemplate not a univer-sity college but a full university, involved in postgraduate study and its own research, instead of being limited to first degree work. But since many of the problems of existing universities relate to their teaching function at the undergraduate level, this is a limitation which has been and must be accepted with equanimity. We must, as I frequently remind my colleagues at Buckingham, see ourselves as a tiny pilot plant on the edge of some vast industrial complex. Anything useful *we* discover, *they* will manufacture and market and take the credit for.

On the financial side it is of course difficult to carry out all the experi-ments one might like to see made. The view that it would be both better for individual institutions and salutary for students if universities charged full economic fees which would then be an important proportion of their income (with the students recovering most or all of the money in the form of enhanced grants) is difficult to test in a single institution, when one is competing for entrants with institutions that can charge very much less for roughly similar courses because they have the advantage of a direct subsidy. Nor can even those local authorities that exercise their option to give Buckingham students discretionary grants be expected to take account of our larger fees. The importance of getting private endowments for scholarships as well as capital costs is thus clear. Meanwhile the high fees clearly distort the basis and hence the comparability of student recruitment. Even with fees at an economic level where current expendi-ture is concerned, it is not possible without intolerable restrictions on intake for us to charge against student fees the infrastructure of buildings, equipment and the original library holdings. This marks a departure from some of the pre-inflation planning when it was hoped that an institution of this kind might be run in such a way as to obliterate the UGC distinction between capital and current account which the founders believed to have been an encouragement to extravagance.

One must add that there is not much so far to be derived from Buckingham's experience in relation to the question of 'student loans' though this was a concept that much interested some of the Founders. If it is hard to persuade students or their families that the advantages of Buckingham for their particular needs justify paying higher fees, it is even harder to persuade them that it would be a good idea to borrow the money, particularly at rates of interest much higher than existed when the scheme was originally discussed in the late 'sixties. It might or might not be a good idea to introduce a loan element into national student finances, but it is not something which can easily be initiated by a single small institution on its own, at least not where school-leavers or other young entrants are concerned. For mature students aware of their own income potential the notion is less off-putting and a modest beginning is being made.

Whether even so, a private institution can realize substantial economies is an important question to which time alone can provide a convincing answer; since accurate budgeting in the build-up period is almost impossible, there being too many unknowns. We certainly believe that our policy of housing students largely in ordinary dwelling houses in units of five or six is cheaper than the once fashionable student hostels, as well as more acceptable to the modern student. But apart from that, the only clear gain is that an independent institution does not involve the State in the overheads that an extremely centralized system inevitably imposes. To get rid of most of the higher education section of the Ministry, and of the twin bureaucracies of the UGC and the Committee of Vice-Chancellors and Principals would be an important saving of non-productive expenditure. If universities were to be entrusted with spending the product of their fees and a subsidy which (apart from research) was calculated on some simple formula, it would probably much increase their efficiency. I suspect there would be ample lessons to be derived from the experience of independent schools who almost certainly get much more out of a given input of funds.

The difficulty of going further than this (apart from it being too early to evaluate the Buckingham experiment), is that academic efficiency is itself much harder to test than efficiency in the production of commodities that are sold in the market. Schools have external public examinations which given all the differences of clientele still tell one something. Universities can only be judged by their products after some lapse of time. Even with external examiners the mere number of first or upper seconds as a proportion of the student body is not an altogether satisfactory indicator — and likely to be much harder to operate where as at Buckingham the age and nationality range of the student body is designedly different from the norm.

On the input side there are two factors which work in opposite directions where economy is concerned. There is first of all the so-called two-year degree course. I say so-called because the term calls up inevitably the idea of two of the conventional British academic years. In fact two calendar years of four ten week terms each produces something near the ordinary number of teaching weeks for the full degree course. If in the case of British school-leavers we include the three- or four-month period spent under the College's supervision following a specially designed language course at a foreign university (a practice we hope gradually to make compulsory), the amount of study-time is in fact greater than that at ordinary British universities. It is a clear economy in that the 'plant' is much more intensively used and of course in an almost wholly residential institution this also applies to its use in the evenings and at weekends. What needs to be watched is whether this pattern involves too many individual problems in the case of students who for ill-health or some other reason miss part of a term and find that there are no long vacations in which to catch up. (The longest vacation is between the two calendar years of study (i.e. from mid-December to the end of January).) There is also the difficulty created by the fact that those who graduate in December cannot enter upon professional courses or most postgraduate courses until the following October though the more enterprising should be able to put this period to better use than is often made nowadays of the conventional long summer vacation; if finance permits we would hope that a number of our graduates would spend part of the time at an American university or college. One will also need time to find out whether a staff that teaches intensively for three terms in four can be as productive in terms of research as one which follows the more normal pattern.

A consideration of effectiveness in this sense leads one to consider the one aspect in which the Buckingham experiment would seem to be less economic than what is done elsewhere, and this is the high priority accorded to face tutorial teaching mainly in groups of four or less. Oxford and Cambridge have traditionally done this even on a one-to-one or one-to-two basis by expecting college tutors to have more 'pupil-contact hours' than is common for lecturers elsewhere. It means at Buckingham an apparently heavier burden than that to which teachers in other universities have become used; although in times of financial stringency the very loose rein over junior staff in particular may well be tightened. Even so, Buckingham's method will only be shown to be economic if the result is to get better quality performance from students of a comparable level of ability or previous preparation and that will take time to find out. It is obviously attractive to students from non-English speaking countries where in other institutions their linguistic handicaps may pass unnoticed until it is too late. But important as are the international aspects of Buckingham and its provisions for the teaching of English to a specialist level in the fields with which it deals, the crucial question is what effect the high-intensity teaching offered will have on British students for whom in the first place, the 'independent alternative' was called into existence. It is particularly important to be able to measure this in the case of mature or post-experience students who always figured very largely in the planning discussions that led up to the creation of the College. How does a highly intensive form of teaching in a tight-knit small community compare for instance with what the Open University can achieve for its own far-flung clientele who have to rely much more on inner motivation?

One difficulty here, as with so much that we are trying to do at Buckingham, is that we have not got the resources in our early years to spend on monitoring our own performance and comparing it with that of others. The verdicts of external examiners will be helpful but by themselves insufficient. What would be needed could be one or two members of staff teaching part-time at Buckingham and part-time at some other institution and keeping a record of the progress of particular sections of comparable student-intakes. So far I have not found a Foundation willing to pay for this, and there are prior calls on our own finances and likely to be for some time to come. The task may have to be undertaken retrospectively at some future date when the importance of our experiment is more widely appreciated.

If it is hard for the reasons given to estimate what contribution the independent alternative might make to re-thinking the nature of the financial arrangements the country should make in respect of higher education in general, it is even more difficult at this early stage to say whether the more intangible benefits claimed for it are likely to prove convincing. Will students who pay for their own higher education or whose fees are at any rate closer to real costs show a different attitude towards their work and the institution itself? Will they be more concerned to get value for money? What form will the natural radicalism of the young take in such an unusual situation — unusual that is outside North America? The small initial intake gives one only a few pointers to what might turn out to be the answers to these questions after a good many more students have been at Buckingham and for the full two years.

It is clear for instance that the fact that our students are paying a greater share of the cost makes them both identify themselves more closely with the College as an institution, and show a greater awareness, sometimes a critical awareness, of how our resources are allocated. It also leads to a more critical attitude to what is offered, a greater questioning of the validity of particular academic decisions and a greater sense of the differential merits of teaching methods, and even of different teachers. All this is on the whole to the good; though the usual impatience and occasional ignorance of youthful enthusiasts makes it a more difficult if more interesting task for the academic administrator than a more conventional student body would provide. The danger that one can see may lie in the fact that an institution of this kind may attract too high a proportion of students whose attitudes to higher education are wholly instrumental. They may too readily reject subject matter that seems to them unrelated to their future professional or career choices, and too easily think that good teaching can be a substitute for, instead of merely an adjunct to, personal study. Would-be lawyers are perhaps particularly prone to attitudes of this kind as are many overseas students. A larger student body with a wider range of academic interests may help to cure a latent tendency towards philistinism which is obviously there in the present set-up.

Two ways of counteracting any tendencies of this kind suggest themselves. The first which like so much else, is largely a question of resources is to provide a greater balance through the development of non-vocational disciplines — history and literature — and opportunities for the arts — notably music. The other method is to try to show the extent to which only a narrow view of the demands even of a professional career would assume the irrelevance of any but technical subjects. We have not found it at all hard to persuade would-be lawyers that the knowledge of European languages can be an asset; can we find ways to overcome their disbelief in the utility of knowing the languages of science and mathematics? In all probability this is linked to another function of any institution of undergraduate education, widening the horizons of the individual in respect of the whole gamut of careers available in the modern world. The national disinclination, so often noted, to regard industry and commerce as suitable areas of activity for the educated, comes into this as well. Here one can only say that our original commitment to building careers advice into the admissions procedure and of not losing sight of students' needs from this point of view at any time while they are with us was obviously correct. If we can do a useful piece of work here it should be of general interest; and the corollary of having students who are rather instrumental in their approach should make this pragmatic approach to the broadening of their interests the most obvious one. On the other hand nothing must be allowed to obliterate the fact that learning for its own sake must always be an essential element in any institution of higher education — public or private — and in all our schools of study provision must be made to bring home the importance of this fact.

It might be worth adding that while there is a clear if as yet indefinable influence upon what goes on academically from the fact that our students are fee-paying, there is almost none from the fact that our endowment is private. Apart from grants earmarked for a particular subject or for scholarships — awarded at our own discretion — all the money we have raised has been given totally without strings. Nothing is indeed more amusing (if sometimes irritating) than the people who ask one whether we have not just replaced dependence on the State by dependence on 'industry'. One can only imagine that those who ask this question don't know many businessmen. If they did they would see how absurd is the notion that they are eager to spend their own or their companies' money in order somehow to influence what is taught in universities or how it is taught. If they have an ideological bias it is to hope that we can show that the spirit of initiative outside the State sector is not wholly dormant; but what we actually do is something left to us. Even the businessmen who sit alongside some of our academic staff, academics from other universities, professional men, and a headmaster and headmistress on our council of management limit themselves very conspicuously to questions of finance and are almost painfully modest about their competence to deal with issues of academic policy. The difficulty is not that the world of business may interfere too actively in our affairs, but that eminent men of business have too little energy to spare from their own primary responsibilities (particularly in these hard times) to give such an enterprise all the attention we should like. There is no private DES or UGC or Comptroller- and Auditor-General. We are very genuinely out on our own.

The problems of student 'participation' and self-organization for extra- curricular purposes are likely to be different at Buckingham, not only because of the different self-image of paying students but also because of the greater age range and higher proportion of non-British students entering with different expectations as well as different experiences to call upon. The main element of difference is however size. Even when we reach our target of 500 to 600 students the College will be very much smaller than any British university. It is true that it will be about the same size as the larger Oxbridge colleges; but the effectiveness of the parallel is limited by the much greater degree of academic autonomy that Buckingham enjoys. An Oxbridge college may decide upon how to handle much of the teaching of its students (less in the case of the natural sciences) and deal with its domestic life on its own; but its undergraduates have to follow courses designed by the university and pass examinations carried out by the university and are even obliged to accept the (now minimal) degree of discipline of the university. An Oxbridge under- graduate might have occasion to deal with the head of his college, he would hardly have occasion to call on the Vice-Chancellor in the ordinary course of business. We have thus had to provide a system of participation which rests upon the accessibility of all teaching and administrative staff, and on the minimum of formality in staff—student relations as well as the maximum of autonomy where non-academic activities are concerned. The whole atmosphere of high level confrontation brought about by the 'recognition' of the NUS, by the DES and by the Committee of Vice- Chancellors and Principals is totally remote from what happens or is likely to happen at Buckingham. At Buckingham membership of the students' union is voluntary and it collects its own subscriptions. One could hope this would be a pointer to developments elsewhere where the present system is, we believe, quite indefensible from both the students' and the taxpayers' point of view. But again it is too soon to try to describe the system that is developing; one can only say that its key concept is partnership within a single community.

I have more than once referred to the non-British element in the student body, and it is indeed in relation to the international role of British higher education that the independent alternative may have some of its most useful lessons to offer. In part, this ingredient was foreseen and allowed for in the earliest planning stages. We always intended to provide for a reasonably sized contingent of American college students spending a whole or part of their junior year with us, and always thought that an institution which began with this notion could do better than those where it is a matter of fitting the visitors into a system designed for quite a different purpose. We would also think that this would be a better contribution to the education of the students themselves and to Anglo-American relations than the 'overseas' campuses that some American universities maintain in ghetto-like isolation from the rest of the British academic community. We also hoped and intended in a newly 'Europeanized' Britain to attract students from Western Europe. What we did not anticipate was the demand from the Third World — largely but not exclusively the Commonwealth.

In dealing not only with the students we have got or have agreed to take in 1977 (who will of course be at Buckingham when this essay reaches print) but also with those we have interviewed and turned down — and we rarely refuse at present to interview a prima facie serious applicant — some conclusions of a provisional kind have already emerged.

The first and most obvious conclusion is that while higher education remains one of Britain's potentially most important exports, we have done nationally very little to investigate the implications of this fact. Hence the imposition of such things as differential student fees which violate both academic decency and the ordinary canons of market economics. Why should customers pay different prices for the same commodity? We have charged and will continue to charge identical fees to all students doing the same courses. Since our fees are necessarily high this may be said to produce once again an intake biased in favour of the better-off. We can only meet this where students are eligible for financial support from external sources. But there seems no real reason why assistance to Third World students to pay proper economic fees (if everyone else does) should not be an obligation upon the Ministry of Overseas Development. It is at least an area in which it has a reasonable chance of assessing the value of what it is doing, and how the British taxpayer's money is being spent. It is absurd that what is essentially a subsidy to certain countries (whether for humanitarian or political reasons) should come out of the universities' own budgets.

The second conclusion is that it is probably the case that too many overseas students are being allowed to *begin* courses of higher education in this country. I say 'begin' advisedly since quite a high proportion of those who apply to us have made a start elsewhere. What has defeated them? Two things essentially. The most obvious is language. Even from Commonwealth countries where secondary education is in English and where a reasonable colloquial level can be expected, one cannot rest assured that the transition to university work demanding the understanding and manipulation of abstract concepts is within the students' immediate reach. Teaching for this specific purpose is needed, and for many such students it should be a pre-entry requirement as we are beginning to make our own experimental course. For those who have never been taught in English the problem is much more obvious and for that reason perhaps easier to identify. The second reason is linked to the first. In any institution which works through a set syllabus by means of large classes with little direct personal contact, it is all too easy for anyone with linguistic or other cultural barriers to fall disastrously behind without it being noticed until it is too late to remedy the situation. No institution doing degree standard work should be allowed to take overseas students unless it takes full responsibility for dealing with their problems through close personal supervision. Some institutions, fascinated by 'growth' have clearly not observed this requirement. It would be far better to halve the number of Third World students we take and spend twice as much effort on each of them. To say 'throw them in at the deep end' is fine for a British sixth-former from a good school. If he sinks, one can usually fish him out. For an overseas student it may mean drowning.

It is because we recognize that we must justify our existence by dealing with the problems of many different kinds of students and can benefit so much from many who fall outside the normal pattern of undergraduate recruitment − the mature post-experience students especially − that independence is so essential to us. It has been and is essential not to be part of UCCA but to insist that we design our own entry forms, use our own tests, carry out our own (often intensive) interviews and choose our students with only the minimum of formal guidelines. Again, to continue to do this involves remaining small. One aspect of the enterprise fortifies another.

It is not only on the student side that independence of action is required. We must be able to select, remunerate and deploy our academic staff − and decide upon their teaching and administrative roles and burdens − irrespective of general rules and conventions. We could not function if we were bound by standard contracts, standard scales of pay, standard ratios of senior and junior staff, standard hierarchies. Nor can we ignore the utility of part-time teaching to vary our offerings whether from the staffs of other universities, the recently retired or the aspirant young. Nor need we, nor do we, restrict our staff any more than our students, to British nationals. If we are to assist the academic community by acting as a pilot plant we must be a little piratical. If there is to be an 'independent alternative' the extent of the independence it requires must be accepted by the rest of the academic community. It must also be accepted by ourselves. The lesson that has been learned by me as a result of the planning period and of the first year of operation, is how hard it is to think and act in defiance of the norms to which one is used. When trying to raise money from senior figures in the world of business, one finds that one has only to mention the word 'university' for them to think wholly in terms of the Oxford or Cambridge of their youth − and mine. Academic staff come pledged to independence and autonomy and insensibly drift into suggesting that the only way to do some particular thing is to do it the way they did it in whatever institution they last worked. How in recruiting staff one detects alongside academic and teaching talent (which is not too hard to spot) the talent for innovation is something one is learning only painfully and by experience. But we need to learn this skill. One thing I am determined to avoid is that the independent alternative should turn out to be 'the same but smaller'; it has in some ways to be better.

Reference

1. For the origins of the idea see the pamphlet by Professor H. S. Ferns, *Towards an Independent University* published by the Institute of Economic Affairs in 1969 (revised edn. 1970) and the book of essays, *University Independence* ed. by John MacCallum Scott, Rex Collings, 1971.

Chapter 8

Developments at the Open University

Sir Walter Perry

The whole of this book is about higher education alternatives. The Open University can be regarded merely as one alternative to the traditional system of higher education used by other universities. But this is altogether too simplistic a view. The Open University is a very complex system within which a large number of sub-systems are interlocked and I have recently described this complex system in detail.[1] Some of the sub-systems involve innovative changes, each of which is in a sense an alternative to a pre-existing practice. Other sub-systems are very traditional and present no alternative whatsoever. Those who are interested in adopting higher education alternatives can seldom if ever take over the complex system of the Open University as a whole, for it cannot be expected to work in different social and demographic circumstances. It therefore seemed to me that I should attempt to identify some of the major innovations inherent in the Open University system, to consider each in isolation from the rest of that system, and to examine how far each could separately be adopted for use in other systems of higher education. My hope is that such an analysis, although messy and blurred at the edges, will be of value to potential innovators elsewhere.

Among the major innovations introduced by the Open University are first, the deliberate aim of reaching the adult or 'mature' learner coupled with the abandonment of any requirement for entry qualifications: second, the integrated use of the mass media of communication in an attempt to rely wholly upon a distance-learning system: and, third, the 'course team' approach to course design.

It is on the other hand important to realize that the Open University is not, in its development to date, an alternative to traditional systems of higher education in respect of the standard of intellectual achievement demanded for the award of a degree or of the basic disciplinary content of a degree programme.

I will examine some of the implications both of the alternatives created by the innovations introduced by the Open University and of the deliberate decision of the Open University not to offer other alternatives by innovating in other respects.

Reaching the adult without entry qualifications

In Britain higher education has traditionally been directed towards the completion of a continuous end-on sequence of initial educational steps, each step being offered to a smaller and more highly selected fraction of the age group. This system is extremely efficient in the sense that it involves very few errors of commission; of those selected to proceed to each sequential stage of initial education the percentage who fail to complete that stage is very small. Thus British universities, accepting less than 5 per cent of the age group at entry, turned out some 90 per cent of the entrants as graduates. The drop-out rate from universities of some 10 per cent was the lowest achieved anywhere in the world. On the other hand it is a system which inevitably involves a large number of errors of omission in that many young people who are intrinsically capable of benefiting from higher education were denied entry to it by the operation of the selection system. In the system of higher education in the USA where some 50 per cent of the age group went to college the proportion of errors of omission was much smaller but, conversely, the proportion of errors of commission was high and the drop-out rate from college approached 50 per cent. Thus, while the US system provided a chance of higher education to many more people it did so at much higher total cost to the nation and at a higher personal cost to those individuals who spent longer on their initial education without being able to achieve their goal.

In Britain the highly selective system has been, in part, eliminated by the post-Robbins Report (1963) expansion of the universities and the polytechnics; and the Open University was a deliberate attempt further to correct the imbalance by providing an opportunity of higher education to those who, for reasons of the selective system or for reasons of personal choice, had not proceeded to the last sequential stage of the initial educational system. In other words it was to provide another opportunity to adults whose initial education had been cut short.

This decision posed a number of questions that required solution.

When the Planning Committee considered those questions in 1967 there was very little evidence to go on. That there was indeed a pool of adults capable of, but denied an opportunity of higher education was unquestionable. But how many from the pool would take the 'second chance' if it were offered? Was the pool a finite one which would rapidly be drained? The estimates of the Planning Committee were necessarily crude. They could have spent years of research, probably abortively, on this sort of 'market research', but they had no time. The miracle is that, with the flimsiest of evidence, the Government agreed to spend large sums of money as an article of faith that the creation of the Open University would be justified by the demand. That the faith was not spurious is now proven by the fact that more than 250,000 adults have already applied for entry; that the pool was not a finite one is proven by the fact that each year the model age of applicants far from rising, as it inevitably must with a finite pool, has actually fallen.

Would the same demand have been forthcoming if the opportunity of a second chance of higher education had been provided through a traditional system? It is impossible to tell. The difficulties of making such provision would have been immense. Most adults are occupied with the basic tasks of bread-winning and child-caring and cannot afford to stop work to attend residential universities on a full-time basis. Furthermore, the nation could ill afford to spare them for this purpose from productive work and from their contribution to the GNP. Could part-time evening classes have filled the gap? Birkbeck College offered such opportunities to those who could reach it, but it was the exception. There was little chance that other universities, already struggling to cope with a big increase in the number of students wishing to embark on programmes of full-time study, would willingly have embarked upon the concurrent introduction of schemes for part-time students. Furthermore, a sizeable fraction of the population lived too far from any university to benefit from such a solution. Then, too, many adults whose initial education had been cut short lacked the self confidence of the school-leaver and feared the potential ridicule of failure. There might be grave problems in persuading them openly to register in conventional universities even on a part-time basis. All in all the prospects for such a solution seemed remote. Nevertheless systems of this kind are being made to work in other countries, notably in the antipodes.

A further difficulty in basing a system of higher education for adults upon traditional methods lay in the fact that it depended upon a standard entry qualification. Thus institutions could validly assume that all entrants to first-year courses had achieved, in the previous year or two, the same minimal level of attainment in the appropriate prerequisite school courses. If the same criteria were to be applied to adults it would either put upon them a burden of preliminary study that was daunting, or it would depend upon the acceptance of qualifications obtained many years earlier when school curricula had been very different so that such adult entrants would in no way be truly comparable to recent school-leavers. First-year university courses intended primarily for school-leavers could not reasonably be modified to their disadvantage simply to accommodate unqualified adult entrants. Thus to provide adequately for unqualified adult entrants demanded a new and separate institution which would not require entry qualifications.

Even then the new institution could face a formidable challenge in designing courses that were suitable for adults; and especially so for adults whose qualifications at the moment of entry would be quite extraordinarily diverse. Indeed there were many in the academic world who believed the task to be impossible of achievement.

The Open University has been, for the last six years, a higher education alternative in this first respect. It is a separate institution offering courses specifically designed for mature adult students (and not, by definition, for school-leavers); the courses have been deliberately created to make it possible for entrants of widely diverse achievement and background to succeed; and to a reasonable extent they do succeed. It has proved that a demand exists from adults for such opportunities and that the pool of adults demanding them is not finite but is continually being topped up. I would thus conclude that the following tentative conclusions may be drawn from our experience.

1. There is no reason to doubt that, among any adult population, there will be a number who will seek an opportunity of higher education. In Britain some 50,000 adults apply for entry to the Open University every year — about 1 in 500 of the population of adults.

   Can other countries then assume a similar rate of demand? I do not believe they can. In a country with a non-selective system of entry to higher education for school-leavers, the pool of adults deprived of that initial opportunity will be smaller. The demand will necessarily depend upon the awareness of the adult population of the existence of the opportunity. On the other hand it may well be that, in developing countries, for example, the motivation of the adult population to secure a higher education may be much stronger, thus increasing the potential demand. Thus our experience does not eliminate the need for a careful assessment of the demand before embarking on the introduction of a similar alternative elsewhere.

2. It is possible, over a considerable range of disciplines, for adults to succeed in higher education even if they start without the entry qualifications normally demanded of school-leavers. This conclusion may be applied to countries which, like Britain, have a system of compulsory secondary school education; it may not apply elsewhere. It is not, however, valid to assume that one can extrapolate this conclusion and expect that school-leavers who are unqualified for entry will succeed in the same way as do adults. They may lack both the life experience and the motivation that come with maturity.

3. It is possible to devise courses that are particularly appropriate to adult learners. Such courses could be used by any kind of institution and by any method of teaching, traditional or otherwise. Courses that are designed for school-leavers are frequently unsuitable for adults, especially for unqualified adults. It follows that it will be very difficult to cope adequately with both types of student in a single class.

4. To devise good courses for adults calls for knowledge, skill and experience with adult learners. It can most satisfactorily be accomplished by staff dedicated to this goal rather than by those whose primary objective is the teaching of school-leavers. There is consequently considerable merit in basing higher education for adults in separate institutions.

Integrated multi-media courses for distance-learning

If the above conclusions are justified it follows that the Open University could have devised courses for adults and taught these courses by traditional face-to-face methods in an institutional setting. It was, however, agreed from the outset that the Open University would be innovative in another way; that it would offer an alternative higher education in a second sense. It set out to prove that distance-learning was a feasible alternative to traditional programmes that depended upon face-to-face teaching.

Various forms of distance-learning had, of course, been tried before. The mass media of TV and radio had been used experimentally, and correspondence education had been widely used; but nearly always with a very heavy drop-out, so that only a relatively small proportion actually succeeded.

When the teaching programmes of the Open University were being developed the basic objective was to try to ensure that all adults in the country would have an equal chance of studying with success. This meant that those who lived in remote places such as the highlands and islands of Scotland must not be disadvantaged by being unable to travel to a centre to meet a teacher; that students incarcerated in institutions, such as prisons or hospitals, must be catered for; and that special arrangements would be necessary to prevent disadvantage to students living in areas where, for instance, the signal of a national network like BBC 2 television could not be received. In turn this meant that, even in urban communities where students could easily turn up for face-to-face teaching, we could offer it only as a remedial measure and not as an integral part of the course. These remedial measures might not be readily available to every student; but all the basic learning materials must be available to everyone. (In fact we now provide remedial tutorials for remote students by telephone.)

Thus the entire basic system was devised as one wholly dependent upon distance-learning aimed at adults working primarily from their own homes. There was only one exception to this general principle, namely that all first-year courses and many later courses, especially those in science and technology, would demand, as a requirement for credit, attendance for one week at a residential summer school. This concession, as it were, to the need for face-to-face instruction was accepted from the outset, largely on the advice of Howard Sheath, who had for many years been responsible for running an external degree programme in the University of New England, at Armidale, New South Wales. This programme, which served principally teachers in the Australian outback, was correspondence-based with no TV or radio. Sheath was adamant that students were retained (some 70 per cent proceeding to graduation) to a considerable extent because they were stimulated and re-motivated by attendance at compulsory summer schools. Since the Armidale record was quite outstanding among correspondence schools, we were determined to follow his advice and adopt this pattern.

All our remaining tutorial provision in study centres is a voluntary activity on the part of students who feel the need for it. No student need attend tutorials. Other than the summer school week, each course relies only upon distance-learning methods.

There was great suspicion in the academic world about the feasibility of doing away with face-to-face teaching. There was also great pressure from our own staff to introduce more and more of it, since they themselves were accustomed to it and knew that it worked. Furthermore, many students enjoyed it and felt, perfectly properly, that it was very valuable. It required continuous vigilance and continuous pressure to avoid using it on an increasing scale. But we could not indulge in it, because to do so would be to make our system extremely expensive, adding the costly media of television, radio and correspondence texts to traditional methods rather than replacing traditional methods by them.

Another feature of the Open University distance-learning system was that the mass media of TV and radio were to be used as adjuncts to a correspondence course and not as the main media of instruction. This was an apparent departure from the initial concept, hallowed by our original name, the University of the Air. It was also at variance with most experiments, mainly in the USA, in the use of educational broadcasting. These experiments had often been promoted more by the broadcasters than by the academics who were contracted to do the teaching; the vision was usually of using broadcasting as the main medium of instruction. This turns out to be enormously expensive in terms of air-time and also leads to the misuse of an expensive medium to convey much that can be conveyed more cheaply and just as effectively through the written word. Thus many educational broadcasts did no more than put a camera into a classroom, instead of using television to do what only it can do, namely transmit a moving video-signal when that sort of signal is needed for strictly pedagogical reasons. Only about 5 per cent of all teaching in the Open University is done through television. Students must read for their degrees. The realization of this fact was a vital factor in gaining academic credibility for our distance-learning system.

Just as soon as it is realized that television time is itself a scarce resource, the use to which it is put becomes selective and thus proper. The same applies to the use of radio as an adjunct to the distance-learning system.

The guts of the distance-learning system used by the Open University is the correspondence package. This consists of a specially written text in the form of what we have called 'structured learning'. It is not fully developed 'programmed learning', nor is it a straight pedagogic text; rather it is something in between, calling for active responses from the student at intervals throughout. The package also includes notes on the related broadcasts, references to set text-book readings, and assignments which a student must answer. These assignments are another vital feature of the system, serving a dual purpose, first of acting as a continuous assessment of the progress of the student, and second, and perhaps more importantly, of being an intrinsic teaching device. The corrected assignments serve to illuminate for the student his errors and misconceptions and are a very necessary feature of his learning. Such tuition by correspondence is an absolutely key factor in the distance-learning system. The aim must always be to secure the quickest possible feedback of corrected assignments to the student; and this in turn depends on an adequate postal service.

The distance-learning system of the Open University was devised without the expenditure of any money on the development of new and sophisticated methods of course distribution. We based our multi-media system upon those media that already existed in Britain in a usable form, notably the BBC national broadcasting networks, the post office, and a high quality local library service throughout the country. What we did do was to integrate the use of these pre-existing distribution systems in such a way as to make the best possible use of each for the pedagogic purpose under consideration. Thus, for example, television time is apportioned unequally between courses, more being allocated to those courses with the greatest need for a moving video-signal. The various messages conveyed by the different media are interlinked by cross-reference and other devices. Each course is designed as an integrated whole.

That our distance-learning system works in practice is now borne out by results. On average 70 to 75 per cent of the students registered for a course gain credit in that course at the end of the year, and this has now been true, with only minor fluctuations, for six years. In that time we have produced over 20,000 graduates who have successfully accumulated six such credits (or eight in the case of those taking honours degrees). Of the first cohort of 19,000 students finally registered in 1971, some 50 per cent have graduated after six years and this number will increase slowly for several more years, for there is no time limit for taking a degree.

It is also true that success is dearly bought. I have often said that ours is one of the most difficult paths to a degree yet devised by the wit of man. It demands of students qualities of motivation, of determination, and of staying power that are perhaps unusual. That it is a possible but difficult alternative to institutionally-based face-to-face higher education is, however, now indisputable.

Perhaps it is then fair to conclude that distance-learning systems could be devised to meet other needs in higher education than those that we have tackled in the Open University, subject to the following provisos:

1. I believe that the distance-learning system of the Open University can seldom be applied directly in other countries. They must utilize the distributional systems that pre-exist locally, and devise their own integrated multi-media mix.
2. I have grave doubts as to whether less mature students, e.g. school-leavers, would succeed as well as do adults in a distance-learning system, but evidence on this point, even in Britain, is still sketchy. On the other hand, it could well be that the intense drive for higher education among the young in those developing countries with few residential university places would significantly modify such doubts.
3. The mass media must be used properly if the distance-learning system is to succeed. This implies control by academics rather than by broadcasters. (I would add that, in the case of the OU/BBC partnership, the BBC producers are academic colleagues rather than opponents, but this is not true in many other countries.)

4. The various media used must be integrated into a coherent course from the start. Attempts to base a written course component on a pre-existing broadcasting component, designed originally for a different purpose, can succeed but are often very unsatisfactory.

The 'course team' approach in course design

Another major innovation of the Open University was the concept of the course team. In traditional universities the common pattern had always been that the determination of the nature and content of each course that was offered to students had been the task of the head of the department concerned; and that each module of the course had been the responsibility of one individual teacher who presented his lecture, seminar, or tutorial to his students behind the closed doors of the classroom. There were two strong reasons why the Open University could not use this traditional system. In the first place all the teaching materials would be open to view on national broadcasting networks or on sale in bookshops. They would thus carry the imprimatur not only of the individual teacher or teachers but of the institution as a whole. Secondly, the average academic had little knowledge of the particular needs of the adult learner, of the problems of distance-learning, or of the best ways of using the broadcasting media.

In consequence our courses were devised and controlled by a team, appointed *ad hoc* by the Senate, and consisting of academic staff, educational technologists and BBC producers, all of whom had an equal voice in determining the syllabus of the course, the method of presentation of the course, and the choice of medium through which each element of the course could best be transmitted to the students. What, then, are the advantages and disadvantages of this new innovative approach, this further alternative in higher education?

The advantages are that the individual idiosyncrasies of teachers are eliminated. There is no place for the dull and uninspiring lecture. The needs of the student tend to have a much higher value placed upon them.

The understandable tendency of some academics to concentrate upon their own particular interest to the detriment of their treatment of other facets of a subject is counteracted. The fact that some courses act as feeders, as service courses for other disciplines, can be accommodated by having representatives of these disciplines as members of the team itself. Above all, many minds rather than only one are bent to the task of devising the best possible course. The fact that Open University courses are multi-media ones is, in a sense, coincidental. The course team approach would offer these advantages whatever the method of presentation.

On the other hand there are significant disadvantages. The most important is that the process is both lengthy and expensive and can be justified in economic terms only when the resulting course is to be offered to a large enough number of students to reduce the cost per student to an acceptable level. This can be accomplished within a single institution as large as the Open University. Smaller institutions can only achieve it if they share the financial burdens — if the courses produced by one are used by many. This is by no means an attractive prospect to many academics who tend to believe that no one can devise as good a course as they can; and who, moreover, may be concerned, especially in times of financial stringency, with a real fear of redundancy.

There is also a very real loss of academic freedom implicit in the course team approach. No one individual can teach exactly what he wishes; he must carry the team with him. This does not necessarily mean that individual points of view are necessarily lost; but a polemical approach in one segment of the course material will normally be counterbalanced in another segment by the presentation of the alternative view. Nevertheless, the system could, as I have pointed out[2], be used for propaganda or for sedition especially when it commands the use of the mass media.

Despite the disadvantages I am firmly convinced that the course team approach has led, in the Open University, to the production of high-quality courses. This conviction is reinforced by the fact that they are currently being used in their original form, and in translation, in a large number of other institutions in many countries throughout the world. I therefore believe that we can draw the following conclusions:

1. The general standard of higher education courses would be raised by the wider adoption of the course team approach to course design whether the teaching is carried out by traditional or by non-traditional methods.
2. This improvement can, however, be achieved in a traditional university only if courses are freely interchanged. Otherwise the costs are likely to be prohibitively high. If courses were so interchanged, they could be offered by a system of independent self-paced learning with further savings in cost. Even if the use of pre-prepared courses of this kind were restricted to 'core' courses the cost-effectiveness of higher education as a whole could be considerably enhanced.
3. In the development of distance-learning systems the course team approach will be an absolutely necessary feature of its success. The involvement of the producers of broadcasts and of experts in adult education and the problems of distance-learning itself are as crucial as the strictly academic input.

The 'standard' of degree courses

The Open University accepted from the outset that there would be no compromise on the standard of intellectual achievement to be demanded of students taking undergraduate courses leading to the award of a degree. This was considered, for very good reasons, to be absolutely essential for an institution otherwise so innovative and experimental. In the first place a degree of inferior standard would be of little value to graduates seeking employment, even if it were a valuable education in itself; and, secondly, the whole concept of distance-learning in higher education as a viable system would never have been accepted by the academic world if the degree had been perceived as an inferior one.

Nevertheless, the deliberate decision not to compromise on standards, not to offer any alternative in this respect, had serious repercussions. The language used by the teachers makes no concession whatsoever to the limitations of vocabulary of the more deprived and less qualified entrants. Indeed one of our graduates, asked in a television interview about what books he had consulted most frequently, replied 'an English dictionary' because he had been unfamiliar with so many of the words used in the teaching materials. This was clearly an additional handicap to his, highly successful, study; it is almost certainly a handicap so heavy as to make the study of many such students unsuccessful. The foundation course teams had not been unaware of this problem and had tried hard to choose language that would not impose such disadvantages, but it was an extremely difficult task and clearly we were not wholly successful. The hard fact is that abstract concepts can only be discussed through the use of words that are not in common everyday use and that are consequently unfamiliar to many intelligent but educationally deprived adults. Consequently although we might, with extra time, effort and resource, do more to minimize this disadvantage, without dropping the standard, we probably can never eliminate it.

A further and more serious repercussion of the decision not to compromise on standards is that it makes our form of open learning closed to that segment of the adult population which is intellectually unable to achieve the required standard. Yet the standard is itself an arbitrary one which varies widely throughout the world. The fact of the matter is that, in Britain, the standard is fairly uniform in all universities. Fluctuations are minimized by the use of external examiners as monitors. They are also minimized by the uniform remuneration of staff imposed by the UGC on all universities. There is a wider divergence in the innate ability of the student population in different universities than there is in the quality of staff, in the quality of teaching, and in the standard of the examinations. Thus, the graduates of the prestigious universities are 'better' mainly because those universities attract a higher proportion of the most able entrants and not to any great extent because they teach them more efficiently or demand more of them.

The uniformity of the standard for a degree in British universities is by no means matched in all other countries. There are, for instance, enormous fluctuations in standards among universities and colleges in the USA. Furthermore, the uniform standard in Britain, hallowed by tradition, is a relatively high one by comparison with other countries. It is in this sense that it is arbitrary. There is much to be said for offering qualifications at a lower level of intellectual achievement so as to offer opportunities to a larger number of people. This has been a very strong motivating force behind many of the experiments with non-traditional systems of higher education in the USA, often in relation to providing more adequately for deprived ethnic minority groups.

Such a desire is, in some measure, related to the criticism, often levelled at the Open University in Britain, that it is not adequately opening up opportunities for those adults most in need of help, because it demands too much of them too soon. This has always been a valid criticism. It could possibly have been avoided if the political decision had been to found an 'Open School' rather than an 'Open University'; but it could not, for the reasons I have given, be avoided by the Open University in its early years if it was to gain academic acceptance. Now that it has been accepted, it becomes possible for us to contemplate offering qualifications of a lower standard and this is currently under consideration. Such a move, were it made, would indeed offer another alternative in higher education.

The disciplinary content of degree programmes

For reasons similar to those which called forth the principle to 'no compromise on standards' the Open University also decided that the basic disciplines around which its courses would be built would be those normally represented in similar faculties in other universities; and, indeed, the academic staff were recruited in groups related to each of some twenty-six traditional disciplines. The nature of our foundation courses was multi-disciplinary, each course being designed to act as a re-introduction to the four or five disciplines represented in the faculty concerned. Thus the foundation course in the humanities provided such a re-introduction to the disciplines of literature, history, philosophy and fine art (the last of these embodying both music and visual arts). Furthermore, second-level courses in some faculties were also envisaged as multi-disciplinary in nature; on the other hand other second-level courses were much more traditional in being expositions confined largely to a single discipline. In all cases, however, our original intention was to offer, at third and fourth levels, single disciplinary courses that would vary very little in content from similar courses in other universities.

This was a policy that, once again, quite deliberately did not offer an alternative in higher education. It was open to us to have adopted a wholly different policy such as that of basing our advanced courses not on disciplines but on global problems of peculiar interest (or relevance) to adult learners. We initially eschewed such a policy for two main reasons, first that our academic credibility might have been questioned and second that we knew that many of our students would wish to gain professional recognition of one sort or another to further their career development.

Despite this initial policy we have, as we have gained the academic credibility that we sought, modified our earlier view and we now have, among the courses we already offer or have under consideration, quite a sprinkling of innovatory courses that are problem-orientated rather than discipline-based: and this alternative strategy may well be adopted more frequently in the future.

It has already been seen by the Venables Committee[3] as a necessary alternative strategy for the non-undergraduate courses that may be offered by the university. The Committee laid great stress on the need to develop what it called 'adult concern courses' in which the content would consist of material that adults were involved with in their ordinary day-to-day lives. Such content can, I believe, be treated in an academic way at various levels of intellectual challenge; and can, furthermore, motivate much larger numbers of adults to re-enter the process of education. This is, therefore, possibly the next higher education alternative that the Open University should offer both in its continuing education courses and in its under-graduate programme.

References

1. Sir Walter Perry, *Open University*, Open University Press, Milton Keynes, 1976.
2. Ibid.
3. *Report of the Committee on Continuing Education* (Venables Report), Open University, Milton Keynes, 1976.

Chapter 9

Higher education: no limits to growth?

Professor D. Kallen

The recent history of higher education in Europe has been turbulent. Enrolments in the four major European countries (France, the Federal Republic of Germany, Italy and the United Kingdom) taken together increased from under 1 million in 1960 to over 2½ million in 1970. By now they are well over 3½ million. By comparison, students in higher education in the United States, numbered already in 1960 over 3½ million and were almost 9 million in 1974–75.[1] The smaller European countries went through a similar development. In Sweden enrolments showed a slight decline in the early 'seventies, but only after a rapid growth in the preceding decade. At present they are again on the increase. In the Netherlands the number of students in all higher education grew from almost 84,000 in 1960 to more than 250,000 in 1974–75. In the USSR there were in 1968–69 4½ million students (as against nearly 7 million in the USA in the same year).

Europe has, on the whole, however, not yet caught up with the USA and even not with the USSR for what concerns the proportion of students in higher education as related to the total population. Roughly speaking the population of the four major European countries equals that of the USSR or the USA. The number of students in the four European countries as compared with that in the USSR and the USA is roughly 1 : 2 : 3. However tremendous the expansion of higher education in Europe may seem to the Europeans, and whatever problems this expansion may cause them in terms of cost and of employment of graduates, to name only two major bottlenecks, if we look at the two big world powers, there is no reason to expect that the limits of growth of higher education have been attained. In these two major powers the cost of higher education as well as the employment of its graduates have not led to economic or social disaster. There may therefore also in the European countries be no valid economic or social reason for limiting the further expansion of higher education.

Worry and even alarm over the growth of student numbers have nevertheless in the past year been predominant among educationalists, economists and politicians in Europe.

In various ways European countries have tried to restrict enrolments in their universities and other institutions of higher education. Without much apparent success, if one may judge from the sustained growth of student numbers in almost all European systems. At best candidates were obliged to enrol in other fields of study than in those of their first choice. The appearance of the side-effect of 'parking-area students'[2] in several countries shows, for the rest, how wasteful the 'numerus clausus' policy can be.

There are now signs of a new policy. Its essence is that there should be a place in higher education for everybody who is willing and able, in other words a 'universal access' policy. In the words of the Final Report of the Carnegie Commission on Higher Education this involves 'the guarantee of a place for every high school student who wishes to enter higher education, the introduction of more remedial work, the adaptation to the interests of new groups of students regardless of age, the substantial increase in total costs, and the augmentation of public interest and control' (p. 5). On the European scene, at first sight, an 'augmentation of public interest and control' seems in most countries hardly possible, but it may well be that also in Europe universal access to higher education cannot be achieved without public intervention in the universities' business, in particular for what concerns the necessary adaptation to the needs of new groups of students.

The following contains a number of facts and reflections on the progress of European higher education towards becoming universal access systems in the above meaning.

Growth without limits

Between 1960 and 1980 the number of students in higher education will in most European countries have been multiplied by a factor of three to four. This growth rate need not surprise. In fact enrolments had in many countries doubled between 1950 and 1960 and doubled again between 1960 and 1970. The rhythm of growth has been fairly constant for over twenty-five years and it is likely that it will be sustained for the next decade or so.

Table 9.1 shows the increases in selected European countries. For comparative reasons growth figures for a few non-European countries have been added.

Increases in the non-university sector have on the whole in Europe not exceeded those in the university sector, except for the spectacular growth in the former in a few countries where at the outset no or hardly any non-university education existed. In Japan and the United States, however, growth has been by far highest in non-university programmes.

In the years from 1970—71 until 1974—75 the number of students in higher education has been further on the increase, at a slower rate, however, than in the foregoing decades. Data on the most recent years is, however, more scarce. For a limited number of countries they are shown in Table 9.2.

The OECD Report from which the figures in Table 9.1 were taken, demonstrates (p. 17) this evolution in Europe and in the OECD member countries outside Europe with Table 9.3.

The evolution since 1970—71 in Europe shows a slight trend towards a

Table 9.1 Enrolments in all higher education (1) and in university-type higher education (2), 1950 to 1970 (in '000s)

Country	1950		1960		1965		1970	
	(1)	(2)	(1)	(2)	(1)	(2)	(1)	(2)
Austria	22.5	22.5	38.9	38.5	50.1	48.9	62.5	54.9
Belgium	30.2	20.2	52.0	30.7	84.0	48.8	127.1*	75.1
France	185.4	156.4	256.0	206.2	527.0	434.6	778.8†	654.8
Fed. Rep.	146.9*	122.2	313.2§	257.9	367.4	298.1	494.9	407.1
Italy	240.7	236.2	284.3	276.8	424.7	415.5	694.2	681.7
Netherlands	63.5*	29.7	109.4	40.8	152.6	64.4	229.5	103.4
Spain	113.8*	54.6	185.4	77.1	274.1	125.9	351.9	213.1
Sweden	27.3	16.7	47.9	36.2	83.5	66.2	145.7	120.0
Switzerland	18.3	17.1	30.0	n.d.	35.0	n.d.	43.0‡	38.1‡
Ireland	11.2	7.2	14.0	9.8	20.7	15.4	26.2	19.6
Denmark	19.5	13.1	32.5	14.4	53.2	29.9	77.1	46.1
Turkey	27.7	24.8	65.4	51.2	103.1	66.9	155.4	92.6
UK	294.7	115.2	287.7	146.6	433.4	211.6	589.7†	296.3
Yugoslavia	60.4	54.8	140.6	108.4	184.9	116.3	261.2	180.1
Australia	34.9	n.d.	70.7	n.d.	131.7	n.d.	175.4	n.d.
Canada	167.0	84.7	286.3	145.1	471.3	279.8	711.1†	423.6†
Japan	240.0	224.9	712.0	628.5	1,093.0	938.0	1,685.6	1,406.5
USA	2,297.0	2,079.0	3,610.0	3,156.4	5,570.3	4,725.1	7,608.0	6,124.0

Source: *Towards Mass Higher Education*, OECD, 1974, Tables A, B and C, pp. 54ff. (Definition of 'non-university higher education', *Towards Mass Higher Education*, p. 17 para. 2.)

* Estimate; † 1969; ‡ 1968; § 1961.

Table 9.2   Students in all higher education (1), universities (2) and non-university higher education (3) since 1970—71

Country	1970—71			1974—75		
	(1)	(2)	(3)	(1)	(2)	(3)
Fed. Rep.	410.1	100.4	510.5	626.4	162.1	788.4
Denmark	46.1	31.1	77.2	60.4	41.3	101.7
France	679.3	126.1	805.4	782.9	159.9	942.8
Italy	694.5	15.6	710.1	855.1*	18.0*	873.1*
Netherlands	103.4	126.1	229.5	112.5	149.5	262.1
UK	312.2	286.7	598.9	343.3*	290.3*	633.6*
Sweden	122.7	28.4	151.1	115.1†	22.6†	137.6†
Yugoslavia	180.1	81.1	261.2	252.6	108.1	359.7
USA	6,290.2	1,630.0	7,920.1	6,598.0*	1,921.7*	9,519.8*
Japan	1,406.5	263.2	1,669.7	1,597.3*	309.8*	1,907.1*

* 1973—74; † 1972—73.

Source: *Recent Student Flows in Higher Education* by Ignance Hecquet, Christiane Verniers and Ladislav Cerych, Institute of Education, European Cultural Foundation, Paris, 1976.

Table 9.3   Comparative growth in university and non-university education

	1960—65		1965—70		1960—70	
	European	Non-European*	European	Non-European*	European	Non-European*
University education	8.9	8.6	8.5	6.1	8.7	7.3
Non-university education	9.5	11.9	5.6	11.5	7.3	11.7

* Excluding Australia.

Source: 'Issues and Dilemmas', *Towards Mass Higher Education*, OECD, 1974, p. 19, Table 4.

reversal of the evolution that characterized the twenty years before: non-university education is growing faster than university enrolments in France, the Federal Republic of Germany, the Netherlands. On the other hand, only in Yugoslavia universities continue growing faster than non-university institutions, whereas in the foregoing years this was the case in a majority of countries.

It is too early yet to state this as a long-term trend. Easier access conditions to non-university studies may have, so-to-say, falsified the picture in favour of these programmes. Moreover the creation of new institutions may have affected new enrolments, or, alternately, non-university institutions that were established in the decade before may only have got to a real start in the early 'seventies.

One can safely state, however, that the numbers of students in higher education as a whole will keep growing. In those countries where the expansion of higher education had in the early 'seventies or late 'sixties come to a halt or where numbers had even decreased, such as the United States and Sweden, enrolments have recently again shown an upward trend.

Also, university authorities and policy makers who until a few years ago had constantly been on the conservative side in estimating growth in numbers and in planning for future enrolments, have now abandoned this attitude and plan for strong future increases. In the largest European countries the magic figure of 1 million students in higher education that not so long ago still seemed unattainable, has now become reality or is close to becoming so. This is notably true for France, the Federal Republic and Italy. Relatively speaking, Great Britain keeps lagging behind its three big European brothers, due mainly to the stagnation of growth in its non-university programmes.

A second dimension of the development of higher education that needs to be considered is that of the interaction between growth in numbers on the one hand and increased participation on the other.

The OECD has in its *Towards Mass Higher Education* introduced a distinction between enrolment ratios and enrolment rates: the former refer to the ratio between student numbers and the standard age-group from 20 to 24 years of age, the latter take into account the duration of studies and are based on the age-group to which three-quarters of the students belong.[3]

In those countries such as Denmark, France, Italy, the Netherlands and Yugoslavia, where the length of study considerably exceeds the five-year standard on which the calculation of the ratio is based, the enrolment rate is lower than the ratio. In countries such as Belgium, Sweden and Japan where the actual duration is approximately five years, rate and ratio differ little. In a few countries, notably Australia and, to a lesser extent, the United Kingdom, where the actual duration of studies is less than five years, the enrolment rate is a much more adequate measure of participation than the ratio.

In 1970 enrolment ratios in the European OECD Member countries plus Australia and Japan, varied from 12 to 23 per cent (except for Portugal and Turkey where enrolment was lower). In the United States and Canada they had reached the 40 per cent level. In terms of enrolment rates the first group of countries ranked from 7 to over 22 (the high figure being that for Sweden, where also the highest ratio had been registered). In the second group it reached 30.7 in Canada and 35.1 in the United States. If one leaves out Sweden, however, the European countries only rank up to 15. Hence the application of the more realistic yardstick that the enrolment rate is, accentuates the gap between Europe and North America still further.

Nevertheless, the differences in participation rates between Europe and North America have between 1960 and 1970 been considerably reduced: in 1960 the average enrolment rate for fourteen North-Western and Western European countries was 7.6 as compared with 25.9 for the USA and 19.7 for Canada. In 1970 the same rates were 14.8 (for thirteen countries) versus 35.1 and 30.7. Comparing the group of European countries with the USA, the enrolment rate difference from 1 : 3.4 made place for one of 1 : 2.4.

In fact, in Europe increased participation outranked demographic growth as a determinant of higher student numbers. In the European OECD Member countries growth in the size of the relevant age-group accounted in two-thirds of the countries under consideration for less than 30 per cent of the enrolment increases. In the United States, however, increases were for 60 per cent due to the demographic factor and in Canada for 48 per cent.

The 1970 admission rates to higher education demonstrate that participation in higher education is also in the 'seventies further on the increase. Admission rates as a percentage of the respective age-group for eleven European countries averaged 22.6. Only in two countries were they under 15 per cent and in five countries over 25 per cent.

Growth in numbers and increased participation notoriously affect the social composition of the student body only very slowly and in the long run. The trend towards external democratization is nevertheless clearly discernible. In those countries for which comparative data were available, the proportion of students from the upper stratum of the population decreased (except in Norway), whereas that of the lower stratum increased considerably. The intermediate groups of the population were in some cases on the increase, in others on the decrease. On the whole, the upper stratum students were however also in 1970 still strongly over-represented and those of the lower stratum and, to a lesser extent, those of the intermediate strata (middle stratum and independent stratum), still under-represented. The above data refer, however, only to university education. The OECD report submits on the basis of the scarce data that are available that in non-university education the social disparities are less marked (op. cit., p. 31).

Participation of women in higher education is a further aspect that has drawn attention in the past years. In all European countries as well as in North America and Japan women have increased their share in university education between 1960 and 1970. In most countries percentages have risen slowly, but regularly, but sometimes the proportion of women in universities has shown a striking increase over a relatively short period. In the Federal Republic, e.g., the female participation increased from 20.6 per cent of the total in 1965 to 31.3 per cent in 1970. In Italy the percentage jumped from 26.6 in 1960 to 33.4 in 1965 and further to 38.0 in 1970. In countries with a high initial participation rate of women such as Finland and France, both over 40 per cent in 1960, increases tend to slow down. But growth potential is not a good explanatory variable for the rate of growth: in the Netherlands, for example, female participation marked in 1960 a low 17.9 per cent and had in 1970 only reached 19.7 per cent.

Although in most countries increase in female enrolments is potentially one of the key factors that can cause further expansion of higher education, social and traditional considerations counteract in many countries this potential growth factor.

If one takes into account non-university education, in which notably teacher training and training for the health professions are included, some of the countries with low female participation rates rank much higher. Overall female participation rates were around the mid-'seventies over or close to 40 per cent in Denmark, France, Italy, the United Kingdom and Yugoslavia and close to one-third of total enrolments in the Federal Republic, the Netherlands and Japan.

Female participation in higher education and, even more strongly, the distribution of women students over university and non-university education and over the various fields of study within these two major branches, is obviously strongly dependent on role concepts in the countries concerned. In this respect a gradual breakthrough can be observed in those countries where the share of women in higher academic jobs has traditionally been low. Of the first admitted students to medical faculties around 1973 in Yugoslavia 58 per cent were women, whereas the percentage for Denmark was 46, for Sweden 43, for Japan 37, for the United Kingdom 33, for the Netherlands 27 and for Italy 21. In France the percentage for the latest year for which data are available, i.e. 1965/66, was 37.

From the fact that participation in higher education is still strongly determined by social origin and, though a lesser extent, by sex, no firm predictions as to future growth can, however, be made. The demand for places in higher education depends to a very great extent on the numbers of graduates of secondary education. The level of this transfer is relatively stable. In most European countries it is high to very high and variations up or down are minimal.

Transfer rates for girls are in all countries significantly lower than those for boys. Time-series from 1965 to 1973 or 1974 show that transfer percentages for both boys and girls vary upwards or downwards at the same time. In Sweden in 1965 the rates for boys and girls were 76.6 and 64.5, in 1970 97.0 and 76.0, in 1973 79.0 and 73.7. Higher participation rates of women in higher education have been caused by increases in the girls' percentage in the total of secondary graduates and not by higher transfer rates to higher education.

For what concerns participation by social class the available data do not permit to draw a similar conclusion, i.e. that the increased participation of lower social groups in higher education is a result of their increased share of secondary leaving certificates and not of an increase in transfer rates to higher education. With social selection in secondary education becoming less and less powerful and taking place later and later in the educational career, differential transfer rates to higher education are bound to become increasingly important in explaining unequal participation in higher education by social class. In selective secondary school systems this selection operates at the moment of admission to academic-type secondary schools and in the first years of secondary. In comprehensive secondary systems it is relegated to upper secondary education and to the transfer to higher education. For Sweden the operation of the selection process at the various stages is relatively well known,[4] but because of the scarcity of data and the short life-span hitherto of comprehensive education it is not yet possible to draw reliable conclusions on a larger European scale for what concerns the effect of comprehensive secondary schooling upon the social selection for higher education and upon the growth perspectives of higher education.

The combined effect of trends towards more equal participation by social origin and sex on the one hand, of more comprehensive secondary education on the other, will inevitably mean further growth of higher education. The main lesson that must be drawn from the recent past is that neither restrictive access policies, nor poor employment perspectives for academic graduates have an enduring impact on the further growth of the higher education system as a whole. Their effect is usually, to divert demand for a place in a particular sector of higher education towards other sectors or other fields of study.

The logical conclusion that is to be drawn on the basis of this analysis is that the zero growth point will only be reached when full participation in higher education of the total relevant age-group is achieved. Further variations in numbers will from that moment on be uniquely determined by the demographic factor.

This perspective of universal participation in higher education[5] appears to many scholars and politicians who are concerned about the academic quality of higher learning as objectionable and rejectable. They have, however, on the whole failed to produce concluding evidence as to the decay of academic standards and of academic achievement as a result of widened participation. The argument that the pool of talent has perhaps in a number of countries already for some time, been exhausted and that hence academic achievement is on its way down is as difficult to sustain for what concerns higher education as for comprehensive secondary education. More in numbers does not necessarily lead to less in quality. In the European countries, moreover, the lower social groups have still a very far way to go before they have attained the enrolment rates that the higher social groups had already achieved in the 'fifties, i.e. at a time when the quality of higher education was not yet challenged by the defendants of academic standards. And even if some allowance is made for differences in genetic endowment between social groups, as a result of genetic selection, and, secondly, for negative effects of environmental factors that cannot be counteracted by educational and social policies, there is no valid reason to fear for a lowering of academic standards provided primary and secondary education succeed in offering full opportunities for the diversity of talent, motivations and interests of the total age-group and, provided higher education assumes its vocation of a universal access-system.

Numbers are to be treated with care and to be looked at with suspicion. Predictions of future numbers are to be treated with even greater circumspection. Increases in student numbers in higher education are the result of a complex of factors, some of which pertain to the domain of educational and social policy, some of which are beyond the reach of such policies. It was submitted that in the long term and at the overall level, the latter prevail above the former. It was also submitted that the pressure of this latter type of factors will lead to a further increase in participation. The relevant issue is not whether such further participation is to be positively judged in view of countries' interests, or whether it is desirable in view of young people's personal development, or whether it is compatible with keeping standards of higher education at an acceptable academic level. The relevant question is whether, once participation in higher education having become the experience of the majority of the population, this experience can be made personally rewarding and socially beneficial. In the second part of this chapter a few ideas will be developed on this issue.

Higher education's response to the increasing demand: the case of the Netherlands

The spurious character of the demand for education, as for all social services, has often been demonstrated. Both in education and on the labour market demand interacts with and responds to supply of places. But whereas the supply in schools and universities has an immediate effect on the demand for such places, the supply of jobs on the labour market affects educational demand indirectly. Even in those rare cases where employment forecasts for specific professions are available, their impact on educational demand is diffuse both in nature and in time. Expectations of the future supply of jobs are more often based on the job situation at the present than on the reliable forecasts as to future developments. Forecasts, however reliable or not, may be deliberately used to influence educational demand. They may also be used to conceal the real motivations for curbing or discouraging demand, such as shortage of places in the educational institutions or vested interests of professional groups that wish to maintain or raise their market value by keeping the supply of graduates at a low level.

Planning for higher education, i.e. for specific numbers of student places and a specific output of graduates, in line with employment expectations, is in theory a more adequate and direct means of adjusting the demand for academic jobs to its supply, than a more liberal policy that relies on students' and parents' demand. Its application, however, is fraught with political as well as with technical difficulties. On the whole, planning for higher education as a supplier of planned numbers of graduates needed by the economy, has been a failure. Nevertheless, higher education has to be planned and administered and the employment perspectives for academic graduates will in one way or another, and at one point or another, have to come into the picture.

The Netherlands provide an interesting example of the complexities of higher education policy vis-à-vis the demand for places on the one hand, the supply of places for academic graduates and the perception of the labour market situation by students, parents and academic authorities on the other.

As from 1972 a system of selective admission of candidates to specific university faculties has been in existence. It is in principle a temporary measure, but like most temporary regulations, it has by now become semi-permanent, in spite of periodical protests from the students' associations and in spite of regular policy statements on the principle of open access to higher education for all qualified applicants. A 'numerus clausus' has been applied to specific fields of study, including such fields as medicine, social geography, Dutch and English language. The Dutch selection policy has become widely known because of the lottery principle involved: applicants whose grades obtained in the secondary school-leaving examination do not reach a certain minimum level, an average of 7.5 out of 10 points in the secondary school-leaving examination are given places on the basis of a lottery. Plans of government to apply the chance principle to all applicants (at least in those fields of study for which a 'numerus clausus' exists) have in 1976 been rejected by parliament.

Candidates who have been drawn out, can again apply in the year after, but in full competition with the new generation of applicants. Thus the risk of a cumulative piling-up of candidates has been reduced.

A dramatic gap between numbers of places and numbers of applicants has, however, occurred in a few fields of study only, medicine in particular, e.g. for autumn 1976 1,897 places for an estimated 3,333 applicants, and pharmacy 274 against 482. In some disciplines for which a 'numerus clausus' had been asked, applicants were often less numerous than places available. The conclusion could be drawn that either faculties have overestimated the attraction of their field of study, or that potential candidates have been discouraged from applying and of fear that they might be refused access. Other faculties, to which all applicants are admitted, have to accommodate students who do not wish to risk a refusal elsewhere.

Thus the policy of selective 'numerus clausus' distorts the process of distribution of students over the fields of study according to their prime motivations to their abilities.

In this context it is a euphemism to use the expression 'parking studies'. It assumes that students can, for a while, when places become available, transfer to the field of study of their first choice. In the Netherlands at least, transfer between faculties and between universities is made very difficult by the autonomy of faculties to set their own curriculum. The fiercely defended autonomy of faculties and universities is thus a major obstacle to student mobility and to any rational planning of higher education.

Present admissions policy for higher education in the Netherlands is thus in the first instance a stop-gap device for dealing with the demand for places by secondary school-leavers whose options are at odds with the number of places that are offered in particular in the 'expensive' faculties such as medicine, and several natural science disciplines, and, secondly, in those fields of study whose market strongly, if not uniquely, depends on the number of teaching posts that are offered in general secondary schools.

The faculties play a dominant role in determining the number of places they wish to offer to first-year students. Central government takes the final decision as to imposing a 'numerus clausus' for one or the other field of study, but on the whole its decision follows the recommendations of the universities.

It is not surprising therefore that the frame of reference for restrictive or open access is not so much based on labour market considerations as on the number of places that the faculties concerned have available. And eventually access restrictions are more readily imposed in fields of study where students have to carry out laboratory work than in, e.g. the social sciences. Furthermore, in the latter the political options of students and staff are often incompatible with selective success policies.

Present admissions policy to higher education in the Netherlands must in the view of this author be qualified as short-sighted and as short-term. It is indeed a stop-gap device, a substitute for an adequate functioning of secondary education and of guidance and orientation of students on the one hand, for an adequate post-secondary education policy on the other.

The labour market at large provides an important frame of reference for long-term higher education policy, although it also serves as an excuse for the above-mentioned, rather unfortunate, short-term admissions policy.

In 1960 only 1.4 per cent of the Dutch labour force in the four main categories of occupational activities (agriculture, industry, commerce and transport, and, finally, services) had an academic training,[6] as compared with 2.1 per cent in Sweden, 2.7 per cent in France and 4.3 per cent in Canada. According to a Dutch report, the percentage was in 1960 as low as one (but probably a more restrictive definition has been used than was done in the OECD report in which all higher education was included, whereas in the Dutch data the non-university sector is included under 'semi-higher training level'). In 1970 the percentage had doubled, in 1980 it is expected to have reached the 3 per cent level, and in 1990 the 4 per cent level. Nothing dramatic, though, as compared with the percentage of 'academics' in the labour force that has already been attained in many other highly developed countries. Nevertheless, scholars, committees and politicians alike have periodically been ringing the alarm bell, warning of enormous surpluses of academic graduates and urging for measures to restrict the output of the universities and of the non-university higher education sector.

A leading committee report whose data were presented to Parliament in the 1974–75 session contained information on numbers of graduates on the labour market as compared with the number of jobs available.

In total the academic surplus would in the minimum hypothesis in 1980 be 30,000, or close to one-fifth of the total employed; in the maximum hypothesis this would be 10,000 or 6.5 per cent of the total supply of graduates. In 1990 the maximum surplus would be 130,000 or almost 40 per cent of the supply, the minimum 110,000 or still over a third of the overall supply.

On several grounds such projections have to be interpreted with great circumspection.

First because the surpluses are unequally distributed over the various professions: medicine shows by far the lowest expected surplus, dentistry, veterinary sciences and economics occupy the middle ranges, and all other fields are in the high group, with law topping this high category. The relatively favourable situation in the first and the second group will for a great deal depend on the continuation of the selective entrance policies for these fields of study, but in the case of economics an expected increase in the job supply from 12,300 in 1980 to 20,300 in 1990 explains the favourable position of this professional group. One may, however, doubt whether the expected low increase in the supply of jobs in dentistry (5,600 to 5,900) and in veterinary jobs (1,990 to 2,100) is not an underestimation of the future development.

For most of the high surplus professions, however, high to very high growth in the job supply has been projected and hence the argument of an underestimation would probably not apply. For the other fields such as humanities the low projection (from 10,000 to 12,200) seems justified by the decrease in the school population, a majority of these graduates being employed as secondary school teachers.

Secondly, the projection of student numbers on which the above projections of academic manpower were based, have already appeared to have been too low: whereas the above report foresaw 115,000 students in higher education for 1980, the student population in the Dutch universities had already in autumn 1976 reached 125,000. Interestingly enough, however, growth has been much stronger than expected – in spite of 'numerus clausus' regulations – in medicine studies and in humanities and less strong in, for example, psychology and education. Whereas thus on the whole, the projections as to academic surpluses were based on too low projections of student numbers, the surplus of academic graduates runs the risk of occurring precisely in some of the fields, such as medicine, and also dentistry, that are in the low-surplus group in the above report. One may see in this a failure of restrictive entrance policies – and no doubt it is – but it may also be that the supply of jobs in fields such as medicine and dentistry will in the future be much greater than the above report foresaw. in other words, the demand for medical and dental care will indeed grow much faster than had been foreseen. It may also be that the shortage of medical doctors and dentists that will prevail until and beyond 1980 has stimulated places in medical and dental studies.

At present the unemployment rate of higher education graduates is lower than the average unemployment rate: in 1976 the general rate was 5.5 per cent of the labour force, that for university graduates around 3.5 per cent and that for all higher education graduates around 2 per cent.

It is more than likely that a considerable amount of 'underemployment' of higher education graduates has already been taking place. It is equally more than likely that this process of downward adaptation of job expectations for what concerns the job-seekers, and of upward job-requirements for what concerns the employers, will continue. That would imply that much, if not most of the surpluses that are expected would be absorbed by the labour market by a lowering of expectations of job-candidates and a raising of requirements by employers.

Inevitably this phenomenon has repercussions for the groups in the next, immediately lower qualification range. Over-supply of higher education graduates is, moreover, not an isolated phenomenon. It is expected that over the whole range in the future there will be a shortage of lower qualified and a surplus of higher qualified working force. Table 9.4 illustrates this eloquently:

Table 9.4   Work by qualification level, 1970 until 1990, offer and supply*

	Lower level		Middle level		Semi-higher level		Higher level	
	Supply	Demand	Supply	Demand	Supply	Demand	Supply	Demand
1970	85	86	9	9	4	3	2	2
1980	77	82	14	11	6	4	3	3
1990	68	77	17	13	9	6	6	4

* Estimated, as no reliable data on the number of graduates from non-university education as part of the total labour force are available.

Note: With 'supply' is meant the supply of academic graduates, with 'demand' the demand for such graduates on the labour market.

In a situation of full employment, the shortage of lower-level manpower (5 per cent in 1980, 9 per cent in 1990) will be met by employing higher qualified manpower. In a situation of structural unemployment, it is likely that high-skilled job-seekers are willing to accept jobs below their level of qualification and that employers are willing to hire candidates that are over-qualified. Isolated incidents of refusal of low-skilled jobs to academic graduates are only the exception to this rule. Thus, the structural unemployment will hit the lower-qualified groups more than the higher-qualified, in spite of a reverse situation on the job-market.

The problem has therefore to be re-stated: it is not so much that of massive unemployment of higher education graduates, once it has been accepted that the demand for higher education will continue to grow and that the supply of high-level jobs will not increase at the same rate. The real problem is that of the cost to individuals and to society of a massive over-qualification of the labour force. The possible benefits of massive over-qualification should, however, also be taken into account.

On the cost side the incremental costs of every year of further education weigh heavily in the balance. Whereas in 1975 a pupil in general secondary education cost Hfl. 3,480 a year, the average cost per year of a student in non-university education was almost double and the cost of a student in a university five times higher. Students in the so-called 'A-disciplines' (humanities, law, etc.) cost, however, only Hfl 8,200 a year, whereas their colleagues in the so-called 'B-disciplines' (medicine, natural sciences, etc.) cost no less than Hfl. 36,500 per year.

Furthermore, the average length of university studies in the Netherlands is excessive: in the 'sixties it was approximately seven years and as such only equalled by Denmark. In terms of approximate pass rates (defined as the average proportion of new entrants obtaining their first university degree) the Netherlands ranked lower than Belgium, Sweden and the United Kingdom, but higher than Denmark, France, Italy and Germany.

Apart from training costs graduates may also command higher salaries for the same jobs than candidates with less education. Sometimes salary scales are at least partly based on educational degree, in particular in the civil service sector.

On the benefit side, the optimistic statements of the Final Report of the Carnegie Commission comes to mind:

A college education leads to greater ability to obtain and analyse facts in the process of making (more and more complex) decisions. College graduates tend to act more effectively in the care of their health, in the purchase of goods and services, in the investment of their money, in the care and education of their children ... Going to college generally enhances the ranges of options open to individuals – in jobs, in living locations, in choice of mates, in selection among lifestyles.[7]

The Carnegie Commission is no doubt describing the ideal college graduate. But if only part of these qualities were enhanced by attending higher education, the social benefits would largely outweigh the costs, provided one of two other conditions are met: either an unhampered economic growth, or a dramatic change in priorities, quality of life and happiness becoming more valued than a higher income.

In the Netherlands' educational and social policy of the past few years the optimism of the Carnegie Commission is at first sight shared. The Contours Memorandum[8] states:

Individual development by means of higher education benefits not only the person concerned but society as a whole. If more individuals receive a broader education, there is a great chance that more people will get and keep a grasp of our complex society. If more generous opportunities for higher education are offered, social mobility is strengthened. And economic activity is benefited if we continue to offer vocational courses at the highest level. The first general point of departure is therefore that in principle everyone who asks for it and is suited for it should be admitted to higher education. But there are limitations.

Limitations of an economic as well as of a socio-cultural nature. The distribution of knowledge – one of the three key objectives of the 1973 coalition government of centre-leftist signature, besides distribution of money and power – could be furthered by giving priority to other sectors of education, or the demand for particular fields of study may exceed the supply of jobs on the labour market.

In the translation of the principle of admitting everybody who is 'willing and able' to higher education, the Contours Memorandum, and even a

Memorandum on Higher Education that was published soon after,[9] formulates a number of conditions that in fact severely restrict the right of free admission. Nevertheless, the Contours Memorandum does not exclude the possibility that at some stage between 1985 and 2000 the present US participation rate of 40 per cent would be attained.

A number of criteria are enumerated that can justify restrictive admission to specific fields of study: an unexpected, strong increase in demand, important variations in demand, that would not justify increasing the number of places, shortage of qualified teachers, high costs of particular programmes, etc.

A more spectacular measure to control cost increases of university education is now under preparation. Parliament has voted a law that restricts university studies up to the first full degree (the 'doctoral' examination, comparable to the 'masters' in English-speaking countries) to four years, except for those fields of study to which five years will be granted on the basis of a specific, well-argued request. As could be expected, nearly all faculties in the Netherlands have submitted such requests. But even if a majority would be granted — much against the intention of the law and against the outspoken intentions of the policy-makers — things will never be the same again: the average length of university studies will have to be reduced even in that case to less than five years, as compared with over seven at present.

A further measure by which it is hoped to channel some of the demand for higher education to shorter and cheaper programmes consists in, first, promoting the extension of non-university higher education programmes, at the cost of the universities, and, secondly, in creating a new type of higher education programme that is to provide general education programmes of a relatively short duration. The political climate is, however, on the whole not favourable to the introduction of such new programmes. It is notably feared that they would soon become unpopular second-choice and second-rate options for all those who did not find a place in the existing university and non-university institutions of higher education.

And, finally, in line with the principle stated in the Contours Memorandum that 'everyone must be able to continue learning for the whole of his life and to reorientate himself by training, study, discussion and reflection. Educational facilities are needed for this, facilities accessible to everyone which thus, distributed over time and space. . . .' (p. 154), in line with this principle a modest start will be made in 1979 with an Open University. A Memorandum 'Open University' has been presented to Parliament in March 1977. The costs of this Open University will, according to the Memorandum, be very much lower than those of traditional higher education, and it is made quite clear that apart from other policy considerations the cost factor has played a great role in the decision to create a new, special institution instead of, as had first been foreseen, enlarging the possibilities for part time and evening studies at the existing universities. It is expected that the Open University will, at least for a time, help to solve the dilemma in which educational policy in the Netherlands has increasingly found itself: because of the intolerable burden of higher education on the country's resources,[10] alternatives had to be developed to too costly and too long university studies.

Many of these alternatives will now be developed outside and without the universities. The universities' share in higher education will diminish. The Dutch example may in this respect be a warning for the universities in other countries: they have failed to notice the changing tide. Their seemingly unlimited growth was on the one hand dysfunctional as they were not prepared or not able to offer to their vast new clientele the variety of courses that they needed. On the other hand the political tide has changed: their claim on more and more resources, together with their apparent inefficiency began to meet with hostility among political parties, trade unions and the general public alike. Student unrest and students' extreme political action and stands have contributed to this changing climate. It seems fair to say that as a result the Dutch universities are in a bad predicament. It seems equally fair to say that from a point of view of general interest of the nation it is appropriate that the priorities are now laid elsewhere and that the new opportunities are created without and outside the universities. The opportunity that they have thus missed will not soon return.

Notes and references

1. Comparable and recent data are equally difficult to obtain. For the OECD countries comparable data from 1960 to 1970 can be found on OECD's *Educational Statistics Yearbook* (Paris, 1975). Data as from 1965 until a very recent year have been published in *Recent Student Flows in Higher Education* by Ignance Hecquet, Christiane Verniers and Ladislav Cerych, Institute of Education, European Cultural Foundation, Paris.
2. With 'parking-area students' is here meant: students who register for a field of study in which they are not planning to graduate, but where there happens to be a place, and from which they will transfer to the discipline of their first choice as soon as possible. In the Federal Republic this phenomenon has reached the stage at which its dysfunctions by far exceed its functions. It can safely be assumed that some 30,000 candidates for the medical faculties are at present enrolled in other fields of study. As of these only 2,500 can be admitted to medicine each year, the average 'waiting' or 'parking' time is in theory well over ten years. In practice it has from the winter-semester 1973−74 to the same semester 1976−77 grown from four to six years.
3. *Towards Mass Higher Education*, OECD, p. 23.
4. See Torsten Husén, *Social Influences on Educational Attainment*, OECD, Paris, 1976.
5. 'Universal' is here used in the sense of full, 100 per cent participation.
6. *Statistics of the Occupational and Educational Structure of the Labour Force in 53 Countries*, OECD, 1969.
7. *Priorities for Action*: Final Report of the Carnegie Commission on Higher Education, McGraw-Hill, 1973, p. 13.
8. *Contours of a Future Education System in the Netherlands*. Discussion Memorandum. A Ministry of Education and Science publication, The Hague, June 1975, p. 136.

9. *Hoger Onderwijs in de Toekomst* (Higher Education in the Future), Publication of the Ministry of Education and Science, January 1976 (only in Dutch).
10. In 1977 of a total of over 18 billion guilders for education almost 5 will be spent on higher education (universities alone 3.4 billion).

Chapter 10

Conclusion: present trends and future policies

G. T. Fowler, MP

Are we within or entering a period of revolutionary change in patterns of higher education? It is possible to argue that we are not. The growth and mutation of higher education systems in the post-war period may be seen as resulting from the operation of historic factors. There have of course been some new attempts to resolve traditional tensions or conflicts, and the pace of growth has been faster than in any previous period. But except where the use of new teaching technologies have been possible, there is little that need occasion surprise in the historically aware.

The 1963 Robbins Report quoted Confucius' dictum that it was not easy to find a man who had studied for three years without aiming at pay.[1] While the Report gave less weight than might have been expected to the vocational training which is for many an essential element in higher education, it was right to point out the antiquity of vocationalism in education.[2] The great mediaeval universities of Europe prepared their students for the professions of the Law and the Church. Many of the American land-grant colleges had their origin in the labour needs, especially in agriculture, of the developing States.[3] Some of the English civic universities began in the last century as local institutions seeking to meet the vocational as well as the cultural aspirations of the populace. The vocational emphasis of much post-war policy in Britain, leading to the creation of first the colleges of advanced technology and then the polytechnics, is thus in no way new.[4]

Tension between vocationalism and the demands of scholarship can again be found in previous periods of university development. But it was in the nineteenth century that high scholarship, and then research (not strictly the same as scholarship, but subsumed with it under Robbins' phrase 'the advancement of learning')[5] became as important elements in the total activity of higher education institutions as the preparation of students for subsequent careers. In the sciences, the British saw the rising academic pre-eminence of Germany and feared its industrial spin-off. But the two types of activity were always logically distinct. The policy that polytechnics should be primarily teaching institutions, conducting relatively little research, was thus meant to mark them off from contemporary universities, but did not distinguish them from universities in many previous periods.[6]

It was the nineteenth century too which saw the formulation of the role of the universities as refiners and dispensers to their students of a high culture which marked them off from their contemporaries. It was not the first age in which young men had attended university to be 'finished', but there was a new emphasis on the polish given in the finishing process, not least to the scions of the new hand-hewn industrial aristocracy. This endowment with accepted culture became an essential, or an advantageous, qualification for admission to or advancement in certain careers. The concept of the university as a 'Culture Mart', as Adelman categorizes it,[7] thus spilled over into, and created new tensions within, the vocationalist approach. Scientific and technical studies, which gave the young a practical competence, but left some of them with rough-and-ready social *mores*, became in some circles less esteemed than the humanistic disciplines. The alienation from productive industry which some now perceive in the educational process, the whole of which became ever more influenced by the criteria acceptable in higher education, can thus be seen to have deep roots.[8]

Demand for higher education as a 'job ticket' seems at first blush a post-war phenomenon. But it is the older acceptance of the view that it is the development of the general powers of the mind and the inculcation of the common culture which fit the graduate for desirable forms of employment, that underlies this.[9] Superimposed upon it has been a rapid increase in the proportion of 18-year-olds seeking higher education, an increase partly the consequence of rising general prosperity, partly of better and extended public sector school education, and partly of public financial support for students.[10]

Support for students is but one example of increasing governmental intervention in both the demand for and the supply of higher education. It has nineteenth century origins in financial inducements given to some would-be teachers. On the supply side, financial aid to universities became formalized immediately after the First World War.[11] If it be accepted that aid without guidance, or an open-ended commitment to spend public funds without expression of the public interest, can never be acceptable to governments, then it is clear that recent 'interference with university autonomy' also has deep roots.[12] An alternative strategy sometimes adopted by governments, and not only in Britain, in order to avoid charges of moulding universities to their own purposes, is the creation of new non-university institutions of higher education under more direct public or 'social' control.[13]

It is against this historical background that some current proposals which present themselves as radical changes in the orientation of higher education must be viewed. It is for example certain that the recent demand for 'relevance' is new, but only in its use of the word as if it were intransitive, so that studies could be relevant without being relevant *to* a defined external objective.[14] When the word first came into vogue in the late 'sixties, the denunciation by students of a course as 'irrelevant' seems to have meant that they did not perceive the value of the academic knowledge it transmitted to the transformation of society. Learning for learning's sake was going out of favour with the students before it went out of favour with the politicians, but this was not a demand for the traditional

158   Conclusion: present trends and future policies

vocationalism. That came back into favour with the worsening employment prospects of the 'seventies, and the demand that education in general and higher education in particular should be more relevant to the needs of the 'economy' or of 'productive industry' came first from employers and politicians rather than students, in Britain at least.[15] Equally, it was then too that loud protests were heard that not all those specifically trained for one vocation could obtain employment within it — namely, teaching.[16]

I would maintain that most demands for 'relevance' in higher education envisage less alternative forms of it than its refinement within traditional forms to meet social needs which academics, students, or politicians think they see. The growing popularity of some of the social sciences in the 'sixties was thus related in part at least to the belief that they held the key to the eradication of social ills which it was now possible both to describe and to explain. African studies, Caribbean studies and the like were the recognition that an education designed to meet the needs of one society were not necessarily 'relevant' to those of another, radically different. More broadly, black studies in predominantly white societies embody a realization that a non-unitary society may have differing sets of needs, some of them perhaps incompatible. But these are merely extensions of the principle embodied in the education in universities of a social elite, in the transmission of the common culture, and vocationalism — that higher education should serve the perceived needs of society. None demands a new organization of higher education.

Most such refinements of the content of higher education are as apposite to a static as to a rapidly changing society. The most extreme forms of vocationalism are apposite only to a static society, as our experience with teacher education demonstrates. Here we have been unable to cope rapidly enough with demographic variation, the swing up and down in the number of births.[17] Initial higher education finds other forms of social change more difficult still to absorb, and the more directly vocational it is, the more difficult the process.

Rapid scientific advance, followed by technological and industrial change, mean that knowledge and skills date much more quickly now than in any previous period. Granted the lead time to the production of the first graduates from a new degree course — from the decision to mount the course through the design period, first intake, and the course itself — it should never occasion surprise if some of the knowledge the graduates have acquired is already outdated by the time they come to use it practically. Further, except in conditions of rapid expansion, when new resources are constantly available, higher education must find it difficult to adapt its physical and human plant rapidly enough to meet changing demand. The narrower the specialism developed in the graduate by higher education, the less likely he is to be able readily to acquire a new specialism as his becomes outmoded, since he may lack an adequate foundation of knowledge upon which to build it. Social change, again more rapid than in previous periods, may make fresh but simultaneous demands upon his adaptability, both at the workplace and elsewhere. These problems are exacerbated by greater longevity. Even if the higher education graduate succeeds in adapting and in learning enough to maintain his career impetus throughout a normal working life, he will then face a possibly lengthy period of retirement or semi-retirement, in which new knowledge will again be of value to him.[18]

This is not futurism. The problem is already with us. One possible solution, the lengthening of the period of initial education, makes easier the combination of breadth and specialization; but knowledge will still date quickly. The vocationalist approach to higher education, the belief that there should be a close link between the content of study and subsequent employment, thus has severe limitations, at least if the educational process be seen as belonging to youth alone. Disputes between those favouring broad courses designed to promote the development of the general powers of the mind,[19] and the advocates of narrow studies in depth, can also be seen from a new perspective. At least there must be sufficient breadth to permit subsequent in-service education and training, often in an area of study not covered in the initial course.

It may be argued that these considerations point merely to particular resolutions of long-continuing tensions and conflicts within the traditional form of higher education. But they are rather the harbinger of the gradual adoption of a radically different organizational principle for post-school education. Education must be seen as a lifelong process, with periods of study in parallel to or interpolated between periods of work. The process can continue into retirement. This approach is variously called 'continuing education' or 'recurrent education' or 'éducation permanente'.[20] Its adoption affects the objectives of school education, since for most if not all pupils this becomes the platform upon which subsequent formal or informal learning is built, rather than an end in itself.[21] It affects much more however our conception of higher education. In such a system it need not be normal practice that initial higher education, to first degree standard at least, should take place in youth, nor that higher education once having been completed should be resumed in later life by only a minority of graduates. In devising alternative forms of higher education we are thus liberated from many of the constraints imposed by the end-on-to-life principle.

Changing technology, which underlies some of the difficulties in the vocationalist approach to initial higher education, equally offers a solution to them in the recurrent system. First, it is technological change above all which has made possible a steady reduction in the length of the working week in most jobs. Higher production can be attained with a lower input of human time. Although peaks and troughs of economic activity distort the short-term pattern, the trend to shorter working hours persists and is likely to persist. Greater leisure clearly opens the possibility of continuing part-time study for a much higher proportion of the population than in the past. More significantly, it makes the general introduction of paid educational leave (PEL) a practical possibility for the first time.[22]

PEL may take several forms. The same entitlement to study time away from work may be converted into regular day release over a lengthy period, to successive short periods of release, or to a longer 'sabbatical' period after a given number of years in work. In Britain we have great experience of day release and block release from work to education — but mainly for young people in the immediate post-school years.[23] Although this has normally been treated as a separate issue from the introduction of paid educational leave, it is but a special case of the same general principle. But even in this limited area, our experience has been discouraging. The number of young workers enjoying day release in 1976 was lower than it had been ten years earlier. The Henniker-Heaton Report of 1963, which envisaged a rapid growth of day release, has had far less impact on policy than the contemporaneous Robbins Report, which foreshadowed the great expansion of conventional higher education in the later years of the decade.[24]

The recent history of voluntary day release for young people might thus seem to indicate that there is unlikely to be any general extension of PEL unless there is statutory provision for it. Nor could this simply take the form of the provisions of successive Education Acts since 1918 about day release — that it should become compulsory when the time is ripe.[25] The evidence suggests that the time is never ripe. Even PEL for those teaching in the schools — the entitlement to one term in each seven years for in-service education and training — has been regularly deferred in recent years with the argument that economic circumstances were at present adverse to its introduction.[26] Thus, university teachers remain the only group who enjoy regular PEL. Nevertheless, the concession that in principle at least all teachers should have PEL is significant, since the argument cannot be applied to one profession alone. It is therefore reasonable to look for legislation in Britain, on the lines of that already introduced elsewhere, in the course of the next decade. Granted careful preparation and a low initial entitlement to PEL, the economic disruption attendant upon its introduction would be small. Against it must be set the probably greater cost of failing to re-train and re-educate manpower in a period when new skills and knowledge are constantly demanded.

There are other costs attached to the introduction of PEL than those of forgone production. It may be argued that if the alternative is a structural problem of redundancy and unemployment among the middle-aged, the latter may be disregarded. Perhaps more serious are the direct costs of providing education, and especially higher education, to more students, albeit not of the conventional age-group. They might in the early years be somewhat reduced by the deferment of higher education, or some part of it, by 18-year-olds, releasing spare capacity within the system. At present such deferment is rare, since entry into full-time employment normally forecloses the option of undertaking higher education other than on a part-time basis. But in Britain (and in some other Western countries) spare capacity in higher education may appear in any event. The 18-year-old age-group is at present growing larger with each year, but from 1983 it declines in size.[27] Unless qualified demand from 18-year-olds again increases sharply, as it did in the 'sixties, there must be excess capacity of some 30 per cent in higher education institutions by the early 'nineties. The existence of buildings, equipment, and often staff, reduces even the direct cost of providing institutional higher education for those enjoying PEL.[28]

There is however no reason why much continuing education, even at higher education level, should be 'institutional' in the conventional sense. The second helpful effect of changing technology has been to make possible new modes of teaching and learning which are more flexible than traditional face-to-face tuition in universities. The success of the Open University's distance-teaching, using integrated radio, television, and written materials, reveals the potential of home-based study.[29] Face-to-face tuition is available, but is 'on tap' rather than compulsory, and there have been experiments in the use of the telephone to link student groups and their tutor. Of most significance is not the use of national radio and television networks, the educational utility of which must always be severely limited by the availability of time, but the demonstration that high quality teaching kits of written and audio-visual material (and sometimes simple and cheaply produced scientific equipment)[30] are a suitable vehicle for higher education. Most people can now afford a sound-cassette player. The relative price of video-cassette players may similarly be expected to fall, making them suitable for use in community-based, if not home-based, education.

There is some evidence that distance teaching is more suited to the higher education of adults than of young people who have just left school. It demands more self-reliance and self-discipline than institution-based learning centred upon the student—tutor relationship. It cannot therefore be seen as a cheap method of extending initial or 'youth' higher education. Its utility lies in a continuing education system: it is thus only the adoption of the 'recurrent' rather than the end-on-to-life organizational principle in higher education which can permit considerable expansion of student numbers without commensurate increase in costs. Nor is it reasonable to argue that expansion must in any event be halted, since all those with the potential to benefit from higher education already receive it. There is evidence that the educational process still 'cools out' many able young people before they reach higher education.[31] The recurrent principle entails the abandonment of the 'cooling out' function of traditional educational systems; the objective is to encourage re-entry to education at the level appropriate to the student's learning hitherto, whether that learning has been formal or informal.

For the would-be innovator in higher education a move towards a recurrent pattern of provision has other advantages over attempts to change the institutional structure of 'youth' higher education. When new institutions are created to serve what is seen as a new purpose (often a traditional purpose to which policy-makers wish to give added emphasis), they must contend with the powerful pull of the dominant institutional model within the education system. This is of course normally the university model. Thus, in Britain the former colleges of advanced technology rapidly shed most of the part-time students for whom they had made provision before designation, and sought to broaden the academic range of courses they offered to include the arts and the social sciences. The aim was university status, and the process continued even after it had been achieved.[32] Their successors, the polytechnics, were denied from the outset any hope of being admitted to the university club. While the overall balance of their provision remains significantly different from that of the universities, the same forces are at work.[33] By contrast, recurrent education at the higher education level demands, especially if it embodies some distance-teaching, a radically different organization of courses from the English university degree model. Above all, it must show that 'social responsiveness' which was sought from the polytechnics, meeting the student's needs as they are articulated by himself upon the basis of his work experience.[34]

The difficulty of effecting radical change within the present structure of higher education is well illustrated by the new Diploma of Higher Education. This was to be a broad two-year course of higher education, offering an alternative to the three- or four-year degree, but with the same entry qualification.[35] The problem is that its advantages over the degree course are not apparent within end-on-to-life higher education; for most students it thus becomes merely the first part of a period of continuous study leading to a degree, and for some, the less successful, it offers the opportunity to drop out of higher education with some qualification to show for the study undertaken. Yet within a recurrent education system such a course would have value in permitting the interruption of studies, which could be resumed after further work experience. The stepping-off point thus becomes a stepping-on point too.

Within the present system of higher education most qualifications are terminal in character, and have a value which decreases over time. They mark the successful completion of a defined period of formal study, with success normally measured in part at least by the student's performance in a final examination. They often serve as a passport to a particular form or level of employment, but thereafter career advancement is likely to depend almost entirely upon non-educational factors, above all achievement in the job. In recurrent education the certification of study completed hitherto must look forward as well as back, serving as a guide to what further study might be undertaken later. Further, it is the integration of work experience, informal learning, and formal education and training which should serve as the basis for career development.

One clear implication of this is the necessity of moving away from the system of bald certification now commonly used ('Mr XY has satisfied the examiners in . . .') to a lengthier account of studies undertaken and the level of skill, competence, or knowledge achieved through them. Because studies may be broken, extending over several distinct periods, accreditation is a more appropriate word than certification. Studies may be undertaken under more than one examining or validating body; the evolution of a single standard student record or transcript would clearly ease the difficulties of employers and others in evaluating and comparing achievements.

There are fundamental problems here. The first lies in securing compatibility between credit systems, and it is already with us in Britain. The Open University uses a system wherein six credits at defined levels give entitlement to an Ordinary or Pass degree, and two further credits at a high level to an Honours degree.[36] If one credit is here assumed to be the equivalent of half of an academic year of full-time study successfully completed, this system is compatible with the degree structure of the Scottish universities. It is hard to square with the English—Welsh three-year Honours degree. Nor is it easily compatible with the modular degree structure adopted by some polytechnics for awards validated by the Council for National Academic Awards. There are several different schemes, but the number of modules is not always divisible by six or eight. The spread of modular courses has been given new impetus by the introduction of the DipHE, which is normally so structured.[37] It is thus already desirable that we devise a single accepted credit scheme, or compatible credit schemes.

A second major difficulty lies in securing mutual recognition by academic institutions and validating bodies of each other's teaching, and credits, diplomas and degrees. Attempts have of course been made to establish the equivalence of degrees and diplomas internationally, especially within the European Economic Community.[38] Hitherto they have failed. The task is easier within the United Kingdom; the professional institutions already commonly recognize several different degrees as giving exemption from their own examinations. Against the quaint pretence of the ancient universities that they recognize only each other's degrees and those of Trinity College, Dublin, must be set the discussions about joint validation by two chartered bodies, which have been instigated by the reorganization of teacher education and its division between the university and non-university sectors of higher education.[39] The recognition for credit exemption of studies undertaken under the aegis of another institution, but stopping short of a terminal qualification, nevertheless poses troublesome problems, especially when study has been broken by any lengthy interlude. The credit exemption policy of the Open University offers some guidance, but that remains an internal matter for one autonomous institution.[40] What is required is a national scheme to which all validating bodies will adhere; its evolution must be the task of many years.

The mutual recognition by institutions of the teaching undertaken and of the credits awarded by each other would be a major modification of the accepted concept of the autonomy of universities. In Britain this concept has come to subsume not only independence of the State or organs of Government, but also the freedom to determine academic policy without regard to the views or wishes of other similarly autonomous institutions.[41] The acceptance of a *concordat* about the recognition of appropriate studies for credit exemption, binding upon all the bodies signatory to it, erodes this latter freedom. So too would the use of teaching materials outside the institution at that time having academic responsibility for a student. But that might be essential if a wide range of written and audio-visual materials suitable for distance, as well as face-to-face, teaching were to be provided economically. While a choice of materials dealing with the same subject-matter would remain academically and educationally desirable, the independent production of all such materials by every teaching institution would make any system of recurrent education which included a large distance-teaching component economically impracticable.[42]

Collaboration is thus an essential feature of a recurrent education system, just as competition was the inescapable ethos of the expansion of conventional higher education in the nineteenth and twentieth centuries, when in Britain at least promotion to university status was a primary objective for many non-university institutions.[43] Collaboration between teachers is also necessary when studies are broken, and above all if there is any element of distance-teaching.

In the evaluation of a student's learning attainments, and in guiding him or her to the next stage of study, the teacher presently responsible for him must inevitably be dependent on the judgement of others. This may be contrasted with the extreme example of independent teacher assessment embodied in the traditional pattern of higher education, the Oxbridge scholarship examination. Here the major determinant of a would-be student's acceptance or non-acceptance for a course of studies is his performance in a single competitive test assessed by those who will teach him if he is successful. This is of course an excellent system of selection for elitist 'youth' higher education, where one hidden objective is to 'cool out' some even of those students who have so far surmounted the hurdles placed in their path. It is inapposite to the much wider system of youth higher education with which we are now familiar. In this an element of personal assessment by the future teacher, the interview (of doubtful reliability), remains, but he is largely dependent on assessments made by others in the GCE examination, which performs the 'cooling out' function. In any re-entry system it would be impossible to rely consistently on any recent examination at all. Assessment must be based primarily on previous educational performance, perhaps some years earlier, the judgement of those responsible for the student at that time, and an evaluation of his development since then. To this evaluation the student himself, his employer or his colleagues in the workplace may all contribute. The task of the teacher, as adviser as well as assessor, thus becomes more rather than less complex by virtue of his dependence on the judgement of others, no longer mediated through an examination marking scheme to which we attribute an objectivity it may not fully manifest.[44]

Where distance-teaching is used, the teacher responsible for resolving the student's difficulties, for evaluating and guiding his progress, and for providing moral support to him when he needs it, is not always or often likely to be the same person who devised the primary teaching materials.

In the Open University, those who provide face-to-face tuition and counselling are very rarely members of the team responsible for the production of the course.[45] The course team system means that in any event almost no material emanating from the university is the unassisted work of one person; the work of every academic is subjected to the critical scrutiny of his peers before it reaches the student. Both of these practices are a sharp break from the pattern of teaching traditional in higher education, in which the individual teacher prepares his own teaching materials, even if after discussion with colleagues, and uses them in conclave with his students but in splendid isolation from his colleagues. The collaborative production of teaching materials and their critical examination and amendment by academic colleagues makes possible, without guaranteeing, a consistently high standard of production. This is essential to the success of distance-teaching, where the student may be for periods without either contact with fellow students or access to alternative sources of academic advice. Similarly, the distinction between the teacher as producer of teaching materials and the teacher as face-to-face tutor and adviser must often be inevitable. Thus, the traditional independence of the teacher in higher education from his colleagues can no longer be maintained unchanged in such a system.

Recurrent education also requires new attitudes in the learner as well as the teacher − or if not new, at least attitudes not always found in students in conventional higher education. Not only is he more dependent upon his own resources of character, but he must also, if he is to profit from such a system, seek to integrate formal education with informal learning from experience. In the traditional higher education model, the student may have little relevant experience upon which he can draw, and even in sandwich courses the integration of the practical with the theoretical is not always achieved. By contrast, in recurrent education formal courses must be learner oriented, in two senses. First, the student must, with guidance and advice, be allowed to exercise considerable choice as to what he studies and how, provided of course that academic and educational standards are maintained. He is the only 'expert' on his own past experience and future needs. Second, and in consequence, teaching materials must consist of components or modules small enough to permit student and teacher together to design a package which may in total be new, but coherent and suited to the requirements of the individual. Even the Open University presently offers students blocks of teaching material too large to satisfy this criterion.[46]

It follows from this that in recurrent education courses may consist in part of pre-packed teaching materials (written and audio-visual), and in part of face-to-face tuition, whether in the group or arranged individually. The proportions of each component will vary from course to course, and sometimes from student to student. Each system may be used in one of three types of location. Some teaching, which may be to full-time or to part-time students, will take place in higher education institutions, but there is no good reason why this should always be traditional face-to-face tuition.

A decision on method must turn on the relative effectiveness and relative cost of the alternatives. Some 'teaching' will take place in the student's own home, and this must utilize primarily pre-packed materials, although telephone contact with a tutor may provide some substitute for face-to-face contact. But other teaching and learning may be located within a community building, whether or not it is mainly devoted to education (a school or college or teachers' centre), or has another principal function (a library, community centre, or town hall).[47] The multiple use of existing facilities will be essential to the economical provision of recurrent education. Nor is there anything unduly radical about the proposal; it is already familiar to the extra-mural departments of universities and to the Workers' Educational Association. Teacher and students may travel to the community building to meet together, or it may be the centre at which home-based students meet to discuss common academic problems, or it may be the store of learning materials or equipment which cannot for financial reasons be replicated in sufficient quantity to permit distribution to individual students.

Within this last type of learning location must be included the workplace. It may feature more in courses at a lower level, but we should not disregard the value to some higher education students of ready access to sophisticated equipment, nor of the exemplification in practice of theoretical concepts. This is merely an extension of the principle embodied in the sandwich course, although the integration of practical and theoretical study may be closer. But the successful use of the workplace as a learning location demands the recognition that education and training are not separate activities, but the same process with varying content. It demands similarly acceptance of the complex and continuous interaction of education and employment, which is at the heart of the recurrent education concept, and would replace the traditional view that education services employment. It requires access for the teacher to the workplace, and sometimes his location within the workplace, of the student.

It will be apparent that the adoption of the recurrent education principle postulates not only a change in the roles of the teacher and student, and in their relationship, but also a softening of the boundaries of the institution, not least because its activities may be conducted, and its teachers live and work, away from its main site. Equally, when its students are of mature years, sometimes with a high level of educational attainment, and often learned in the lessons of practical experience, it may be difficult to retain a government structure reflecting the concept of the 'self-governing community of scholars'. Student participation in university government is already familiar,[48] but within recurrent education teacher and student will be more nearly equal, each able to contribute to the knowledge of the other, and each similarly able to take a useful part in policy-making. Even the research function of universities, hitherto the preserve of dons and their favoured *alumni*, may take on a more participatory and simultaneously a more practical hue. The student's lack of theoretical knowledge equal to that of his teacher may often be balanced by his wider practical experience, and his continued involvement in industry, administration, or community activity. In such a system, our universities would of necessity be very different from those we now know.

I have argued that most proposals for change in the content or institutional structure of higher education do not provide alternatives to the present pattern, but rather represent renewed interest in or emphasis on one of the historic themes in university development, albeit in a new form. On the other hand, recurrent education is an organizational principle which makes quite different demands of institutions, teachers, students, and the community, from those made by the traditional end-on-to-life educational system. It is unlikely that these demands can be satisfied in the near future. But early discussion of them, and of the means of meeting them in practice, is desirable. Our present system of higher education has evolved by drift and by policy accretion: it is the result of centuries of 'disjointed incrementalism'.[49] Paradoxically, the more diffuse structure required for recurrent education can never emerge save as the result of careful and collaborative planning.

References and notes

1. *Higher Education* (The Robbins Report), Report of the Committee appointed by the Prime Minister under the Chairmanship of Lord Robbins 1961–63, H.M.S.O., London, 1963 (Cmnd 2154), para. 25.
2. The Robbins Report, 'the ancient universities of Europe were founded to promote the training of the clergy, doctors and lawyers.' But thereafter the Report is lukewarm about vocationalism, asserting merely that it does not involve a 'betrayal of values'. On the mediaeval universities in England, cf. V. H. H. Green, *The Universities*, Penguin, Harmondsworth, 1969, pp. 7–20.
3. See e.g. L. Cerych, 'Le concept de fonction de service public des universités', in *University and Society*, de Tempel, Bruges, 1974, pp. 63–72.
4. See T. Burgess and J. Pratt, *Policy and Practice*, Allen Lane, London, 1970; T. Burgess and J. Pratt, *Technical Education in the United Kingdom*, OECD, Paris, 1971; E. Robinson, *The New Polytechnics*, Penguin, Harmondsworth, 1968.
5. The Robbins Report, para. 27. Cf. C. Carter, in *Patterns and Policies in Higher Education*, Penguin, Harmondsworth, 1971, pp. 77–8.
6. *Plan for Polytechnics and Other Colleges*, White Paper, H.M.S.O., London, 1966 (Cmnd 3006).
7. H. Adelman, *The Holiversity*, New Press, Toronto, 1973. Adelman seeks to divide higher education institutions into four types: the Sanctuary of Truth; the Sanctuary of Method; the Social Service Station; and the Culture-Mart. The classification is perhaps more directly applicable to North American higher education than to European.
8. See *Educating our Children*, Department of Education and Science, London, 1977.
9. The Robbins Report, paras 26 and 28.
10. During the 'sixties in Britain the proportion of 18-year-olds entering higher education nearly doubled to more than 14 per cent. Cf. R. Layard, J. King and C. Moser, *The Impact of Robbins*, Penguin, Harmondsworth, 1969, pp. 13–25.
11. The University Grants Committee was established in 1919.

168   *Conclusion: present trends and future policies*

12. On the reconciliation of public funding with university autonomy, see The Robbins Report, paras. 725–32; and Report of the University Grants Committee to the Secretary of State for Education and Science, H.M.S.O., London, 1968, paras 552–611.
13. For a discussion of 'social control', see G. T. Fowler, 'Decision-Making in Post-School Education'. Unit 14 of Open University course E221, *Decision-Making in British Education Systems*, Open University Press, Milton Keynes, 1974, pp. 15–21; cf. Fowler, 'The Binary policy in England and Wales', in Universities Facing the Future, *The World Year Book of Education 1972/73*, Evans Brothers, London, 1972, pp. 268–80.
14. Cf. T. Burgess, *Education after School*, Penguin, Harmondsworth 1977, ch. 4, esp. p. 116; and *Education: A Framework for Expansion* (White Paper), H.M.S.O., London, 1972, para. 108.
15. The speech by the Prime Minister, The Rt Hon. James Callaghan, at Ruskin College, Oxford, in October 1976, focused on the service given by education to industry, reflecting grumbling discontent among industrial spokesmen about the attitudes and competence of the products of the education system.
16. Estimates of the number of qualified teachers seeking posts but unable to find them in 1976 varied from 5,000 to 20,000.
17. The number of live births in the UK peaked in 1964, but it was not until 1972 that the Government made it clear that the intake of students to the colleges of education would have to be reduced, and not until the middle years of the decade that the policy began to take effect.
18. With the argument here cf. Michael Fogarty, *Forty to Sixty — How We Waste the Middle-aged*, Bedford Square Press, London, 1975.
19. The phrase comes from the Robbins Report, para. 26.
20. See *Recurrent Education: A Strategy for Lifelong Education*, OECD/CERI, Paris, 1973; and *Recurrent Education*, V. Houghton and K. Richardson (eds), Ward Lock Educational, London, 1974.
21. This is relevant to the British debates of the mid-'seventies about the desirability of a 'core curriculum' and of a 'common system of examining' in the schools.
22. See *Developments in Educational Leave of Absence*, OECD/CERI, Paris, 1976.
23. An account can be found in L. M. Cantor and I. F. Roberts, *Further Education in England and Wales* (2nd edn), RKP, London and Boston, 1972.
24. *Day Release*, The report of a committee set up by the Minister of Education (Henniker-Heaton Report), Department of Education and Science, London, 1963.
25. With the provisions of the 1918 and 1921 Acts may be compared the Education Act 1944, ss. 43–6, designed to ensure the release of young workers to 'County Colleges'. The provisions are now generally regarded as a dead letter.
26. The commitment was made in 1972, in *Education: A Framework for Expansion*, 1972 (Cmnd 5172) paras 60–3. But financially hard-pressed Local Education Authorities were in the five years following unable to find the resources for substantial in-service education and training.
27. Because the number of live births peaked in 1964.
28. Factors here are the run-down in teacher education, and control of the number of overseas students in British higher education (through financial and other mechanisms), as well as the declining size of the relevant domestic age-groups in the 'eighties and the recent slower increase in the proportion of 18-year-olds qualified for and seeking places in higher education. Forecasts of the number of places required in 1981 have shrunk from 827,000 (1970), through 750,000 (1972), 680,000 (1974) and 600,000 (1976) to 560,000 (early 1977). At the same time the potential number of places available for 'general' (non-teacher) higher education has risen, because of diversification of provision in former colleges of education. A change in the rules governing admission of 18-year-olds, or greater financial inducements to them to enter higher education, could of course significantly affect the argument in the text.

29. See Sir Walter Perry, *Open University, United Kingdom*, The Open University Press, Milton Keynes, 1976.

30. Ibid. pp. 102–3.

31. For the continuance of the 'cooling out' process in Britain, see Reports on Education No. 86, Department of Education and Science, 1976, which gives a summary of research by G. Williams on factors determining the continuance in education of 16- and 18-year-olds.

32. Burgess and Pratt, *Policy and Practice*, 1970.

33. For the different balance of provision, see Polytechnic First Degree and HND Students, 1975, Careers Advisory Service, Polytechnic of Central London, 1977. But the status-pull on the polytechnics is well demonstrated by M. Trow, 'Binary dilemmas – an American view', in *Higher Education Review* (1969), 2 (1), pp. 27–43.

34. For 'social responsiveness' see Fowler, op. cit., n. 13, 'Decision-Making in Post-School Education', and for the general argument Burgess, *Education After School*, 1977.

35. *Education: A Framework for Expansion*, 1972, paras 110–13; and *Guidelines for Diplomas of Higher Education*, report of a study group established by the CNAA and the UGC under the chairmanship of Sir Walter Perry, 1973. On the entry qualification, see Burgess, op. cit., pp. 150–1.

36. Perry, op. cit., pp. 53–75.

37. Burgess, op. cit., p. 105 and pp. 147–59.

38. See especially *Methods of Establishing Equivalences between Degrees and Diplomas*, UNESCO, Paris, 1970.

39. Most significant may be discussions between the Council for National Academic Awards and the University of Wales, which could lead to the establishment of what would amount to a unified professional qualification for education students in Wales.

40. Perry, op. cit., pp. 152–60.

41. This does not of course imply that within the public funding system universities are wholly free to do as they wish; see the Report of the University Grants Committee, 1968 and Fowler, op. cit., n. 13, 'Decision-Making in Post-School Education', pp. 10–15.

42. The Open University is sometimes criticized because some of its course material is held to present a biased view: see e.g. Julius Gould, 'Scholarship, or Propaganda?', *Times Educational Supplement*, 4 February 1977, p. 20. The case for centralized production of some 'core' materials is made in *Report of the Committee on Continuing Education* (the Venables Report), Open University, Milton Keynes, 1976, especially paras 73–7.

43. Cf. Burgess and Pratt, *Policy and Practice*, 1970, n. 4; and the Robbins Report, esp. paras 419–20 and para. 444, recommending 'some further elevation' of colleges to the status of universities.

44. See J. Pearce, *School Examinations*, Collier-Macmillan, London, 1972, pp. 44–5.

45. Perry, op. cit., pp. 76–120.

46. Not normally smaller than a 'half-credit course', i.e. one-twelfth of an Ordinary degree, deemed to be about 160/170 hours of student work.

47. Cf. Draft *Report of the Commission on Post-Secondary Education in Ontario* (the Wright Report), The Queen's Printer, Toronto, recommendations 17–20.

48. See E. Ashby and M. Anderson, *The Rise of the Student Estate in Britain*, Macmillan, London, 1970, pp. 138–49.

49. This concept of policy development is discussed by D. Braybrooke and C. E. Lindblom, in *A Strategy of Decision: Policy Evaluation as a Social Process*, Free Press of Glencoe, New York, 1963.

Notes on contributors

Max Beloff. Principal, the University College at Buckingham and Fellow of St Antony's College, Oxford. The most recent among his many publications include: *New Dimensions in Foreign Policy*, Allen and Unwin, 1961; *The Future of British Foreign Policy*, Secker and Warburg, 1969; *Imperial Sunset*, vol. 1, Methuen, 1969 and *The Intellectual in Politics*, Weidenfeld and Nicolson, 1970.

Pierre Dominicé. Lecturer in Education at the University of Geneva. Has published in the fields of youth values, evaluation, knowledge and self-management.

Gerry Fowler. Formerly Minister of State at the Department of Education and Science, Co-editor of *Education in Great Britain and Ireland*, Routledge & Kegan Paul, 1973 and *Decision-Making in British Education*, Heinemann, 1973.

Brian Groombridge. Director of the Department of Extra-Mural Studies, University of London. Author of *Education Today* (with Edward Blishen), BBC, 1963; *The Londoner and his Library*, RICA, 1964; and *Television and the People*, Penguin, 1972.

P. Holroyd. A member of the Research and Development Laboratories at Pilkington Brothers Limited.

D. B. P. Kallen. Professor of General and Comparative Education, University of Amsterdam. Author of *Curriculum Improvement and Educational Development* (with G. Papadopoulos), OECD, 1968; *Development of Secondary Education: Trends and Implications* (with A. Little), OECD, 1969; and *Recurrent Education: a strategy for lifelong learning* (with J. Bengtsson and A. Dalin), OECD, 1973.

D. J. Loveridge. Concerned with systems and futures problems at Pilkington Brothers Limited.

Sir Walter Perry. Vice-Chancellor, the Open University. Author of *Open University*, Open University Press, 1976.

Gordon Roderick. Professor in the Department of Extra-Mural Studies, University of Sheffield. Author and editor of many publications in education.

J. J. Scheffknecht. Technical Director, Agence Nationale pour le Développement de l'Education Permanente. Author of *Le Métier de Formateur*, Council of Europe, 1971; *Typologie des Formateurs d'Adultes: Clarification des composantes d'un Système de Formation Continue des Adultes*, Council of Europe, 1974 and *Formation Continue des Adultes, Education Permanente et Société*, Council of Europe, 1977.

Michael D. Stephens. Robert Peers Professor of Adult Education at the University of Nottingham. Author and editor of many publications in education.

Ronald Tress was Master of Birkbeck College, University of London, from 1968 until 1977, when he became Director of the Leverhulme Trust. Previously, he was for sixteen years Professor of Political Economy in the University of Bristol. Among other present offices he is a Development Commissioner and Secretary-General of the Royal Economic Society.

Rt. Hon. Dr Eric Williams is Prime Minister of Trinidad and Tobago and a former distinguished university academic.

Index